STAND UP TO
POLITICAL
BALLYHOO

Also by John P. Gawlak

A Voice in the Village Square

When Memories Nudge You Softly

STAND UP TO POLITICAL BALLYHOO

PLUS
MILESTONES
AND
MEMORIES

John P. Gawlak

iUniverse LLC
Bloomington

Stand Up To Political Ballyhoo
Plus Milestones and Memories

PRODUCTION ASSISTANCE
Carol Gawlak
Charles Gawlak
Kim Gawlak

COVER ART
Charles Gawlak
Kim Gawlak

iUniverse books may be ordered through booksellers or by contacting:

iUniverse LLC
1663 Liberty Drive
Bloomington, IN 47403
www.iuniverse.com
1-800-Authors (1-800-288-4677)

ISBN: 978-1-4759-9136-9 (sc)
ISBN: 978-1-4759-9137-6 (ebk)

Library of Congress Control Number: 2013908949

Printed in the United States of America

iUniverse rev. date: 07/24/2013

For the fallen children and teachers at Sandy Hook Elementary School.

"To think of thy eternity of sleep,
To know thine eyes are tearless though mine weep."

Phillip Bourne Marston

"We must make our choice: we may have Democracy, or we may have wealth concentrated in the hands of a few, but we can't have both."

Louis D. Brandeis
Adviser to President Woodrow Wilson,
later to become a Supreme Court Justice.

WHY I SPEAK OUT

The President has clashed with Wall Street, which indicates that the finance industry has effectively captured our government. The wealth gap is enlarging, and the sharp increase in the power of economic elites is growing. Facing going over the fiscal cliff is indicative that our parties are perceived to have failed our nation, and the crises that afflict us: culture conflict, un-payable debt, illegal immigrants, gridlock in the capitol, and possible defeat in war, may prove too much for our government to cope with. Patrick J. Buchanan, in his book, "Suicide of a Superpower," asks "What happened to the country we grew up in?" The tilt in U.S. policy, favoring the rich, is stunting America's economic growth, aided by how Congress ignores public opinion. This is indicative of the huge disparity in income between the executive class and the rank and file.

OUR HEROES

"Be steadfast, my boy, when you're tempted
And do what you know to be right;
Stand firm by the colors of manhood,
And you will overcome in the fight.
"The Right" be your battle-cry ever,
In waging the warfare of life;
And God, who knows who are the heroes,
Will give you the strength for the strife."

Phoebe Cary

A WISE OLD BIRD

A wise old owl sat on an oak;
The more he saw, the less he spoke;
The less he spoke, the more he heard;
Why can't we all be like that old bird?

Edward Hersey Richards

CONTENTS

A CALL FOR A THIRD PARTY

In Mark Drought's opinion piece, "It's Time to Throw the Bums Out—All of Them" (Advocate, 12/9/11), he bemoans the failure of the deficit-reduction of the super committee. He goes on to say that both parties care more about ideology than fiscal responsibility and have chosen partisanship over patriotism. He calls this "uncompromising extremism" that makes responsible governing impossible. He suggests a solution by calling for a third party for the upcoming 2012 elections.

Our country has a long history of third parties. The first third party candidate appeared in the 1808 election won by James Madison. George Clinton of New York ran on the Independent Party gathering 6 electoral votes. On 1848, Martin Van Buren would run in the Free Soil Party getting 200,000 votes. Abraham Lincoln would win the 1860 election with 1.8 million votes, but he was hard pressed by the third party candidate Democrat Stephen Douglas who received 1.3 million votes. Eugene Debs would run under the Socialist Banner in 1908, 1912, and 1916.

The biggest third party vote getters would be George Wallace (American Independent) with 10 million popular votes and 46 electoral votes. Ross Perot ran under the Independent ticket in 1992 against Bill Clinton. He gathered close to 20 million votes. Others trying to crash the party, J. Strom Thurman under the States Rights Party, better known as "Dixiecrats," Jesse Jackson with his Rainbow Coalition, and Ralph Nader and the Green Party. The 2000 election proved to be the most controversial since the United States Supreme Court had to decide the winner. Al Gore would complain Nader's votes deprived him of the Presidency.

The most recent development is a group of Wesleyan Grads calling themselves "Unity 2008" have banded together to advocate a third party to challenge the long dominant two parties in power. They feel the honorable call to politics, to make the right decisions for the common good, has been vaporized by inter-party fratricide. They claim when government becomes so big as to become beyond the consent of the governed, you reap unashamed corruption and trillion dollar deficits. Based on the premise that all citizens have reasonable expectations that the people they elect will transcribe the will of the people, they have set out on a course of change. Fed up with the ugly unproductive partisan warfare, "Unity 2008" is determined to rise up and do something about it. Refreshing, isn't it?

THE GOVERNOR'S PROPOSED BUDGET CUTS AWAKEN MEMORIES

One of Governor Dannel Malloy's proposed budget cuts is the elimination of the Connecticut Valley Hospital Fire Department located in my former hometown of Middletown. While I was growing up, it was named the Connecticut State Asylum, a huge campus, situated on a hill overlooking the Connecticut River. It was the state's central treatment and confinement center for the mentally ill.

All the buildings were constructed of brownstone, the major construction material of that time. It was mined from the quarries in Portland, a small town across the river. Many of the buildings in New England (town halls, libraries, hospitals, universities, factories, home foundations, bridge piers) were constructed of brownstone. It was shipped by barges to New York City, and by rail throughout New England.

The whole asylum was originally secure, encircled by a six foot high fence of sharpened cast iron bars. The entrance gate was the only opening manned by a guard. All the wards had barred windows and screened porches from which you heard screaming, yelling, cursing and crying. The most interesting section of the asylum was the facility for the criminally insane. For exercise, they were led into a circular, heavily barred courtyard we called the "bullpen." When we were kids, we would gain access to the grounds through the open farmland. We would observe them, some in strait jackets, others performing weird acts of behavior, hoping they would never escape. It still exists.

They grew all their vegetables and raised livestock: pigs, cows, chickens. Sometimes we would play "wiseacres," go where the pigs were grazing, and yell "Sooiee!! Sooiee!! Pig, pig, pig!!" In a stampede, they would come running and squealing, thinking the call was feeding time. We had to jump the fence to keep from being trampled.

It all changed in the 1960's. Mental health advocates convinced the courts that treatment should be community based in group homes. When you walked down Main Street, you would encounter groups of released patients, straggling disheveled, with little sense of where they were. Even the supervisors were indistinguishable. Since this happened, all fences have been removed. The unoccupied buildings, unused for years, fell into disrepair and were demolished. New buildings were constructed and are now mainly drug detoxification centers. The locals now call the facility a "junkie haven."

That institution has made my former hometown groan in agony many times. One escapee set many downtown buildings on fire, including the church of my youth built by Polish immigrants. It was totally destroyed, including irreplaceable stained glass windows imported from France. Another patient would rape and murder a therapist in an isolated treatment area. A local church group is petitioning the state for the release into their custody, a patient who killed his wife with a baseball bat. The mayor and the common council are strapping on their helmets to fight this. By far, the most agonizing incident happened when a patient made it downtown, purchased a knife at a hardware store, and slashed to death a ten year old girl.

My former hometown was also the site, since abandoned, for the Connecticut Reform School for Delinquent Girls, formerly named Long Lane. Under much opposition, the state has recently constructed a $50 million detention center for delinquent boys. Furor has been constant. The former scandal sheet (Bridgeport Herald) had dubbed Middletown the "Dumping Grounds." The weight of history and the emotional wreckage of tragedy rest heavy on my mind. If you can spare a week, ask me about it.

STAY AT HOME IN CHOOSING NEW SUPERINTENDENT OF SCHOOLS

The city stayed at home in choosing the new Chief of Police, Robert Nivakoff. He came up through the ranks, and he has proven to be a wise and honorable choice. The Board of Education is faced with a similar situation in its search for a new superintendent of schools. They are preparing to go on a nationwide search, which I find to be unnecessary, since we have a local very qualified candidate in Assistant Superintendent Winifred Hamilton. She will be appointed Interim Superintendent while the search is being conducted. Winifred Hamilton is a very capable candidate, having served our school system for decades as a teacher, coach, principal, and assistant superintendent. She knows the demographics of the city and the school system, and like the police chief, has an advantage over bringing in a candidate who knows neither the city nor the system, and requires years of acclimation.

The interview process in search of a new superintendent is time consuming and expensive. We have the best candidate in house in Winifred Hamilton. Forget the interim designation. Give her the position because you won't find a more qualified candidate. She was an excellent teacher, an excellent coach, an excellent principal, and she will now make an excellent superintendent.

HORNY BUBBA RIDES AGAIN

This is a story about "Horny Bubba" Clinton, but let's review history that perhaps is indicative of where sexual waywardness had its origin.

Sidney Zion, retired syndicated columnist, coined the phrase "Yakahoola" of noted national figures exposed in extra-marital affairs. And they were plentiful (Presidents Roosevelt, Kennedy, and Clinton; Ted Kennedy, Newt Gingrich). The creation story instituted marital sex, as Adam and Eve were told to multiply and fill the Earth. But the serpent convinced Eve that it isn't all work and no play. So it became fun time, which the Man said was a no-no. Told to hit the bricks, our first parents saw the Garden turn into a swamp. Sex on the side was made peccant, and the ubiquity of carnal desire blankets humanity still. The latest, General David Petraeus, our top military commander, succumbs to the call of the concubine.

But the story of the day (N.Y. Daily News, 11/28/12) is of "Horny Bubba" Clinton stumbling again on the sexual trip-wire. He dodged a bullet with his dalliance with Monica Lewinsky. Jennifer Flowers, one of horny Bill's early salacious forbidden fruit, says old Bill tried to renew a roll in the hay, seventeen years after their original carnal coupling. He was recovering from bypass surgery, and I assume he was eager to test his rejuvenated prowess. She waved him off and told him to get lost. She still looks dashing in her recent photo in the N.Y. Daily News, and states she has become a cougar dating men twenty years younger. Perhaps "Horny Bubba's" magic ripple still simmers. But Flowers says, "Your wicky dipping has gone the way of the tumbril."

MEMORIES OF A VALIANT SHIP

It was interesting to read the article, "New Pearl Harbor Memorial Bridge Dedicated," (Advocate, 6/24/12) and the comments made by some Navy veterans in attendance. Jack Stoeber of Milford, who was stationed aboard the USS Whitney on December 7, 1941, commented how he manned an anti-aircraft gun during the attack. I was 15 at the time, but joined the Navy when I turned 17, and would board the USS Whitney at Noumea, New Caledonia and head for Guadalcanal. We would follow the invasion forces as they progressed up the Solomons, onto New Guinea, the Admiralty Islands, and finally the Philippines. While at the Admiralty Islands (Manus, Los Negros), a Japanese suicide submarine (a Kaiten) snuck into the harbor and blew up the ammunition ship the USS Mount Hood. The fireball was such a huge cauldron that no trace of the ship or the crew was ever found. Damage to ships within a half mile was indescribable. I would later learn that five friends of mine from my hometown were lost with that ship. We were in Leyte Gulf when the war ended, gearing up to join the occupation forces in Tokyo Bay. Veteran crew were given the option to stay with the ship or head home. Don't even ask what choice I made. The Whitney returned stateside after a year, then was stricken from the rolls and scrapped.

A GARLAND IN THE GARRISON

Open homosexuality in the armed services has always been proscribed. The recent repeal of "don't ask, don't tell" is yet to be propitiated. It is an opus that the premise of tolerance and equality is wholesome and refreshing. We have heard from the top that this will be a gilding for the grunts who face enemy fire "outside the wire." Perhaps in officers' quarters where life is discreet. But what about amongst the troops in the trenches, and in close quarters of the barracks? This is a discretionary entitlement for "gays" with no serious regard to merit or consequences. If recruitment is stifled, it has dire implications in the ranks, as it will put the entire military on life support, as it creates a new military culture.

Syndicated columnist Cal Thomas and Sen. John McCain warn that this repeal will cause an alarming troop retention problem, as large numbers of personnel will leave or retire. The president and his cadre of poseurs need to be reminded that the constitution defines and limits their powers. That the polemical assumption that abnormality is morally neutral is harmful. Most Americans today never had a military experience, therefore they cannot comprehend the consequences of "don't ask, don't tell." But the fire of public argument is smoldering, and when full realization is stoked, the crucible of opposition will be forged when the Pentagon starts ordering pink curtains.

Perhaps these anecdotes from the history of homosexuality in the U.S. Military will surprise and awaken you. President John Adams worked to have sodomy (and rum and the lash) removed from our young republic naval branch. It was endemic in the British Navy. George Washington not only forbade open homosexuality in the military, but punished those who practiced it.

Plato wrote, "Any change except to eliminate an evil, is an evil." With this in mind, Patrick Buchanan, referring to the practice begun in the 1960's to allow homosexuals into seminaries, recently said in response to the repeal of the ban, "Let us hope this works out better for the Marine Corps than it did for the Catholic Church." We all know what "gay" priests have done for the church.

DUMBING DOWN PRESIDENTIAL ELECTIONS

George Will, noted syndicated columnist (9/20/12), chides President Obama and challenger Mitt Romney for their grade school responses to the recent outbreak of Middle East violence, "It would require exquisitely precise intellectual calipers to gauge which idea is silliest," writes Will. He states, "Many voters will be astonished by, and even be grateful for, the novelty of being addressed as adults." In life, especially in our politics of past presidents (Nixon, Carter, Clinton, and the Bush's) has led to the erosion of the rhythms of life. They all remind me of the definition of an appeaser: one who feeds the crocodile hoping it will eat him last. They all tinker around the edges because they lack the prism of truth. Both Obama and Romney lack the maturity required to be prophetic or profound. When they speak, they give us slippery platitudes. After Richard Nixon was elected President, he was asked why he hadn't fulfilled all his presidential promises. He responded, "They were all campaign rhetoric." Yet there was no outcry by the voting public. Why is there no authoritative, received truth that restrains this in our government? Just what has become the core tenet of democracy? In debate, when a candidate flubs, from the opposition we hear the sibilant roar of the beast. Yet when the president mesmerizes the public with his musical oratory, fabricated for political purposes that have no basis in reality, the public pulpit goes silent. We as a nation have become unhinged with a chill inducing national debt, two long term wars, high unemployment, and a shaky economy. We need a president who will reclaim the ordinance of "We the people" as prescribed by our Founding Fathers; to bond together in triumph of the human spirit. How long must we wait?

NUNS UNDER SIEGE

In a recent article in the September issue of Connecticut Magazine, the Vatican crackdown of American Nuns, especially the Leadership Conference on Women's Religious (LCWR) is a surprising and revealing harsh judgment. The Congregation for the Doctrine of the Faith (CDF), once the office of the inquisition, accuses the LCWR of promoting radical feminists themes: gay marriage, contraception, abortion, ordination of women. Many of these nuns are part of the community living at the Villa Notre Dame in Wilton. They work in the most rundown sections of Bridgeport caring for poor mothers with children, mostly immigrant and Hispanic. Their harshest critics are Bishop Law and Bishop Lori. Both were involved in covering up for pedophile priests. Law was forced to resign, while Lori was backhanded by the U.S. Supreme Court after spending over one million dollars of Sunday collections to suppress court ordered payouts. Both should have been called to account by their superiors in Rome. But Rome became an accessory by rewarding them with promotions. Yet Lori and Law have petitioned the CDF to launch an investigation into the LCWR.

In a recent shocker (NY Daily News, 8/31/12) well known and highly respected Rev. Benedict Groeschel came to the defense of convicted pedophile, Jerry Sandusky, stating that the kids are to blame. David Clohessy, director of the survivors network of those abused by priests called Fr. Groeshel's remarks, "Disgusting." Joseph Zwilling, spokesman for the New York Archdiocese condemned Groeschel's statement as "terribly wrong." Rome should bring the hammer down on Fr. Groeschel, and leave the nuns alone.

I am a product of a Polish parochial School taught by the Felician Order during the Great Depression. Central to their teaching was to adhere to the words of Christ. And from the pulpit on Sunday was the admonition to avoid sin. When was the last time you heard "sin" mentioned in a Sunday Sermon?

The nuns have held discussions with delegates from Rome, but are resistant to their mandate, "We'll talk, you listen." There is a stalemate to this issue, and the Pope may have to resolve it. The original twelve were not installed with unchallenged authority. Nor were their successors vested with it. But watch out for spunky nuns who discarded their habits because it made them feel like penguins.

MORE GOVERNOR'S BUDGET CUTS

While reading the list of Gov. Dannel Malloy's state budget cuts, I was dismayed and angered to see the suspension of athletic programs at regional vocational-technical high schools as well as elimination of music, art, social workers, library media, department heads. Students at these schools are predominantly minorities. Hispanics with language barriers need additional funding, not cuts. I was also surprised that that closing of J.M. Wright Technical School here in Stamford did not raise the support from the community to keep it operational.

As a former volleyball referee, I officiated many games at Wright Tech. When they played the N.Y. School for the Deaf, the coin toss to determine first serve was memorable, heartening, and amusing. When they won the toss, you had to be creative, since they possessed little hearing or means of vocal expression. To determine "Heads" or "Tails," I would point to my head, or my seat. This always garnered a laugh from everyone. When they entered a gym at Low-Heywood, St. Luke's, Green Farms, Sacred Heart Academy, and saw I was to officiate, they simultaneously pointed to their heads or seats, and giggled. Win or lose, I'm sure I "made their day."

WHEN GENERALS FALL

General Douglas MacArthur would fall for disobeying orders from his Commander-in-Chief, President Harry S. Truman. General David Petraeus, Head of the C.I.A. and hero of the Gulf War, would fall for a dalliance with the author of his ongoing biography. Rumors had the greatest general since Ulysses S. Grant, General Dwight Eisenhower, slipping around with one of his female aides. Even some presidents had zipper trouble. President Bill Clinton would dodge impeachment over Monica Lewinsky, and F.D.R. and John F. Kennedy would fall to bawdy temptations of the booby bounce. Why can't we open our daily newspapers without headlining a noted public figure taking a bite of forbidden fruit?

John Podhoretz, noted columnist (N.Y. Post, 11/13/12) writes, "We live in an age in which personal expression is paramount, and suppression of desire is considered unhealthy and everyone is affected by that revolution of human conduct." It all started with the fall of Adam and Eve, and the landscape has been littered with libidinous carcasses ever since. I grow dizzy when I see former President Bill Clinton who dodged a bullet over a "roll in the hay" with Monica. He now walks amongst us revered and saintly. He should not be venerated because he stained the Oval Office with reprehensible conduct.

CINDERELLA

The New York Daily News (8/16/12) did a feature on Chelsea
Clinton and her thoughts on family and future political aspirations.
It contained pictures with her parents, when she was a young girl.
Her facial features were common and not very enhancing. But the
photo in the New York Daily News surprised me as to the changes.
Her new beauty reminds me of the knight kissing Snow White
from which she awoke. I would like to meet the skillful artisan who
sculpted the new Chelsea into a modern Cinderella. I love it, and I'm
sure it brings sighs to an admiring public.

We look for the children of former presidents to lead honorable
and productive lives. Many have, some not. Go back and review that
photo of Chelsea in the New York Daily News. It will set your heart
aflutter, and wish her rainbows and dreams, and for butterflies to
alight on her shoulder.

PABLUM TREATMENT MAKING BULLYING A NATIONAL CRISIS

Lacking a forceful response to bullying from school authorities, student suicides continue. The latest, "Cruel Girls Drive Teen To Suicide" (N.Y. Daily News, 1/4/12), tells how Amanda Cummings, 15, was so tormented by bullies, she committed suicide by throwing herself under a city bus. We also find it is prevalent in the military with the bully-fueled suicide of Danny Chen (N.Y. Daily News, 1/5/12). Workplace incidents are yet to be revealed due to bully bosses and associates.

School bullying has gone unchallenged for so long that it has become deadly and expansive. President Barack Obama would call a national conference at the White House to explore the issue and seek solutions. I had expected the president to be forceful and decisive. Issuing directives to all bullies to halt their fear inducements or the consequences will be swift and compelling. Instead he was full of mushy lamentations (Bullying is not a rite of passage).

I wrote in this newspaper (Op Ed, 2/5/10) how determined neighborhood kids had the resiliency and courage to solve a schoolyard problem. Of my experience with a bully 65 years ago, and how he was schooled in proper behavior. My eldest son, "Casey," 35 years later, would teach a bully menacing his kid sister right here in one of our local schools, the principles of effacement. In the Navy during WWII, I would engage the ship's bully on the fantail and drop the anchor on him. As seen above, that family practice continues.

We are seeing a proliferation of anti-bullying advocates, publishing and lecturing to school assemblies with proven guidelines to eliminate the plague. To me, their proposals and recommendations are the equivalent of David bringing down Goliath with a marshmallow.

Restraining bullies is not a choice but a duty. Steely grit trumps timidity. Why is this so hard to comprehend? You do not talk a bully down no more that you can talk a cat down from a tree. The bully must be made to feel the sting he administers. This is his/her adjudication. My first grade and kindergarten grandchildren are being taught to strip the bark off bullies they encounter. A blue steel deterrent. Call me a dinosaur but do not question its effectiveness.

15

PRESIDENT'S CHANGE OF MIND

When are we going to get a president that delivers the words of our Founding Fathers intact and without distortion? It surely were not the Bushes or the Clintons. And Obama is catching up. This subject is same sex marriage.

The tragedy of the commons, which is the idea that self-interest can undermine the common good, is the spawning grounds of odious politics that has become the earmark of Washington. The nature of influence is not a chain reaction of virtue. The dimension of honest governance, as old as Adam, has become so askewed, we no longer know what kind of a nation we really are. We did until the 1960's, when the Hippies spilled off our campuses and gave birth to the erosion of American life and values from which we are yet to recover. They still rattle on like lonesome whistles on well worn tracks. The guardians of exactitude, whose patrimony nibbles away at the boundaries of statesmanship, are now regular guests and advisors at the White House.

But it was a "slip of the lip" by Joe Biden that forced Obama to change his mind before he planned to, in endorsing same sex marriages. Like former president Jimmy Carter, Obama states it was his children who convinced him to take this stand. My assessment is that presidents who rely on their children to determine major national policies, is a drift into the cuckoo's nest. The issue is so divisive it may cost him reelection.

HILLARY'S DEFEAT

Just where was the point of departure from Hillary's certain victory to an unexpected crushing defeat? Was it over-confidence? Did she misplay her hand? Or was it, as in other cases of major upsets (sports, politics, wars), when the momentum changes, it is difficult to reverse?

Hillary is lovable but she does carry some baggage. It wasn't that people did not want to see her in the White House, they did not want to see her husband Bill and his access to interns.

There will be many books written about why she lost a sure thing. But let me give you my assessment. Hillary's failure is still about her moral cowardice over Monica Lewinsky. Seeing Bill is a constant reminder. Being coy, about not knowing—she was the only person in Washington that didn't—and then, not taking Bill to the woodshed, this defined her wooly morality. She soon wrote a million-dollar book about her intrepid recovery from being "Wronged," but in reality, she sold her birthright for a mess of pottage. She gave a twinky response to her devastating betrayal.

The press is full of divine honors about her toughness during the primaries. But you must question her toughness in dealing with her "old man." You want to know something? If she threw the scoundrel out in the beginning, you would've seen a new Hillary. America would have rallied to her courageous stand, and she would now be on her way to the presidency. The bumbling Republicans left her a bowling lane.

She vitiated her honor to indulge her ambition, when all signs were nudging her to "shun the serpent's tooth." This put no good will in the bank for her future. No interest to draw on later. Popularity does not trump the essential elements of leadership.

I would like to ask one more question. Why did she allow Bill to run wild as her barker? He was nothing but "storm winds stirring." She would have done better putting Chelsea out front saying, "Elect my mom, she will make a great president." Now that's a dream team.

Said the Devil to Faust, "In the end you are exactly as you are." All that is left is for her to weep in the dark for her requiem. The sobbing you hear is Bill's not Hill's. And America is relieved.

SIGNIFICANT NEWS

With the Mid-East about to unravel, most of us by-pass the headlines to find comfort in the sports pages. Our value quotient is the coming Super Bowl, not the dire consequences of the Egyptian crisis. Do you know the N.Y. Daily News reports that it takes 2000 cows to supply the NFL with enough leather for a season's worth of footballs? Now that is significant news. You see, public taste dictates what is considered newsworthy.

Speaking of the Super Bowl, rummaging thru the attic for some keepsake sports memorabilia, I uncovered a notebook (long considered discarded) from a Humanities course that was required at my university (1950-55). This is not to sound snooty, but after perusing, if you can't enter the conversation about Aristotle, Plato, Socrates, then wandering in the desert should make you feel comfortable.

Aristotle states, that politics is the highest of the practical sciences. The men of Washington go one better: they claim it is salvific. After Christ and Socrates (both good and just men) were publicly tried and executed, Plato in later years would ask, "Is there a city in which the philosopher and the prophet would not be sacrificed?"

We are compelled to testify to the truth, especially when it is unpopular. But as seen above, it sometimes leads to the ineluctable fate of martyrdom.

INDEMNIFICATION OF 9/11: WHEN?

Webster's New World Dictionary defines indemnify thusly: To repay for what has been lost or damaged. Do you know the death and destruction of the Twin Towers, Pentagon, and attempt on the White House has not been indemnified? We have been engaged in 10 years of war in search of the perpetrator, but he has proven to be slipperier than a Connecticut River eel. We know who he is and where he might be, but we have been unable to flush him out of his cave.

We had a similar situation at Pearl Harbor. After four years of a harder war, we got the perpetrator and made him pay. We have the greatest array of fire-power and the most sophisticated intelligence yet we cannot find the cave holding our prey. If there is a reason why we don't want to dig him out then we should be told.

Years ago I read a book review by a retired CIA operative stating they had Osama Bin Laden in their gun sights, but then President Bill Clinton forbade them to pull the trigger. I dismissed this at the time, but as "Slick Willie" got slicker, chickens came home to roost (Monica, Whitewater, Marc Rich amnesty, missing CIA portfolios, etc.).

The full story of the JFK assassination has never been revealed. For our claim of an open society, we have a lot of shuttered entryways.

Former president Jimmy Carter, in a recent article in USA Today (9/30) says polarizing partisanship has frozen government. And big money power-brokers have become too influential in legislative decisions (he calls them "legal bribes"). But he is optimistic that the genius of democratic system is self-correcting and believes constructive governance will ultimately emerge. The last sighting of the prediction was in George Washington's first term.

Our sitting president, Barack Obama, was elected on the resounding promise of CHANGE. But CHANGE has been scarce and "good news" even scarcer. HE has the words, but his magic wand has short-circuited. WE all need and desire to see his promised change come to fruition. Match up your deeds to your silvery speech so that we can all cheer. But massive debt creation (in the trillions and climbing) is the bilge water that will sink his hope for a second term.

If you had the power to spin the magic wheel, who do you see as the next Paladin riding over the distant hill on a white charger waving a new scroll stating: <u>FOLLOW ME!!!</u> Haven't we had enough Don Quixote's?

UCONN GETS STIFFED

Michael J. Hogan resigns as President of the University of Connecticut after serving just three short years. Changes in university administrators usually are the result of incompetence or malfeasance. His reasons were neither. He just decided to go home. Home being the University of Illinois.

Being interviewed for the UConn presidency, the search committee saw in him eye-candy so salivating, they swallowed plates full. His resume knocked their socks off. So impressed they skirted Governor Rell's request that three final candidates be interviewed. When hired, do you know he demanded an office more opulent than President Obama's? Having an allergy to mold, his wife demanded a new million dollar residence be built. Forget mold abatement; new must do.

David Halberstram, responding to what he felt was the central question about Vietnam said, "How so many smart people could have been so wrong." He could have been talking about the blind hiring of Michael J. Hogan. And Aesop wrote, "Beware, lest you lose substance by grasping at shadows." I think Mr. Hogan just got fed up with his slippery and cunning athletic director and men's head basketball coach frequently getting caught in the NCAA's hen-house.

MY FATHER'S WISDOM

How do you respond when put to the test? Adam and Eve lost
paradise for forbidden fruit. Judas sold divinity for thirty pieces
of silver. Brutus slew Caesar for perceived ambition. George
Washington forsook the presidency because of despoiling
partisanship. Grant allowed Lee to keep his sword for the sake of
national unity. John Wilkes Booth assassinated Lincoln to preserve
secession. This was most egregious because Lincoln had a plan
to rectify slavery. Forty acres and a mule would empower former
slaves to be entrepreneurs; to become inclusive to economic, social,
and political fabric of a growing nation, stifling a century of racial
turmoil. Roosevelt and Churchill would rally us to stop Hitler and
Tojo in their quest for world domination. Four brothers and I would
play a part to keep freedom alive. Just how often do the non-descript
nudge their way into history?

In the 60's, we as a nation changed dramatically (for the worse
in my estimation) as the "Hippies" stormed off our campuses
as a drug-crazed mob. A disheartening revolutionary event that
destabilized the structures of certainty that shaped our lives and our
culture. Lincoln said, "There is no grievance worthy of redress by
mob rule." He meant, how do you engage in evil to produce good?

We have a president whose speech lends to the rhyme of a poet.
But his fulfillment is not commensurate with his verse. Mistrust
is seen as a political virtue. Recall the sheer force of high decibel
volume of anti-Palin miasma dispensed as intellectual fungicide. And
it goes on still. Do you know the frailty of our society emerges out
of the depths when given a public forum?

Partisan rancor has turned our citadel of government into a
Saturday night brawl. Coming home late one evening, wearing a few
facial dressings, my father put his arm around my shoulder and said,
"Nobody wins medals by being the toughest guy in a bar-fight." My
father's wisdom never sleeps.

HE'S BACK

The fascination of national politics, is the sway, when whatever party ascends to control. They shed the mantra of a "dour rejoinder." The watchword is change and the concupiscence of success. The party in power reaps the political profits, while the opposition becomes visceral and replete with errant logic. Overwhelming negativity can sometimes backfire, leading to efficacious powers of atonement. We have seen this in the criticism of former President Harry Truman who was sometimes called an "uneducated country boob." Yet he presided over some of history's greatest moments: the decision to drop the atom bomb on Japan that ended World War II; the removal of General Douglas MacArthur for presidential insubordination; and the ordering of the Berlin Airlift that stifled the Soviet attempt to European recovery.

We are seeing some similarities in our local politics: the pros and cons of the Joe Tarzia saga. He has gone from the respected financial watchdog to being bumped to the dog house for overzealous gum-shoeing. Normally, these individuals head to a retreat, write their memoirs and, if they are lucky, appear with Barbara Walters in a soft-soap interview. No sir. Not Joe. He's coming back to put the gloves back on, and scare the hell out of common council members that ran him out of the arena.

UNITY 2008: THE NEW POLITICS

Do you know why we really need change in our national politics?
Because the simple virtue of telling the truth is absent. The
honorable call to political service, to make the right decisions for the
common good, has been vaporized by inter-party fratricide.

The great truth is that very little truth comes out of the political
realm of our nation's capitol. The Gospel of anti-violence was born
here, yet more violence to the truth is committed here than anywhere.
Jesus always prefaced his remarks with "in very truth I tell you."
Arthur Schlesinger wrote, "The truth that comes out of Washington,
regardless of the party in power, is not a cure, but a dodge." This
dishonesty has filtered into plagiarism by noted authors, and into
resume writing. Michael Worthington, Editor of "Resume Doctor"
says, "The broad implication of all this lying on job resumes, I see a
society that's not valuing the truth." This truth twisting, wherever it is
found, mutilates the spirit of our great nation, and renders dissolute
the God-founded legacy of our historical beginnings

A group of Wesleyan grads calling themselves "Unity 2008"
have banded together to advocate a third party to challenge the long
dominant two parties in power. Based on the premise that all citizens
have reasonable expectations that the people they elect will transcribe
the will of the people, they have set out on a course of change.

Noting the growing evidence that Americans are fed up with the
ugly, unproductive partisan warfare served up by Republicans and
Democrats, "Unity 2008" is determined to rise up and do something
about it. The organizers plan to use college students and the Internet
to mobilize millions of disappointed voters to nominate a third
ticket, and engage the existing power structure.

The latest evidence that the public is disgruntled comes from
a poll commissioned by organizers of "Unity 2008." It comes on
top of scholarly research showing 74% of voters are dissatisfied"
with the way the country is going, and 72% say they would like a
wider choice than just the GOP and the Democrats. "Unity 2008"
is a sounding call to action. If you count yourself among the voters
growing disgusted with party lines, learn more about this movement,
and get involved.

NOTES ON OUR NEXT PRESIDENT

The 2008 presidential election is still dominant news of the day and will be for the next two years, even though we have had interruptions of the Imus firing, the killings at Virginia Tech, and the U.S. Attorney General Senate hearings.

The war grinds on in Iraq, and we all groan under the increasing casualties, both civilian and our military. It is easy to become fatalistic under these circumstances, and grumble about the loss of command. I've always held that the verdict is not in, but I find it harder and harder to hold onto that belief.

The reason we are there (weapons of mass destruction) has proven untenable and I find myself asking, "Is the wheelhouse unmanned?" Am I wrong in stating that this war has been poorly planned, managed, and conducted? Which leads to the subject of leadership. Our successful wars have been led by generals, giants in strategy, tactics and resolve (Washington, Grant, Pershing, Eisenhower, MacArthur). Can you name a general of note in this war?

Let's look at the leadership vying to write the next chapter of our national history (Hillary, Obama, Edwards, Dodd, McCain, Giuliani, and others). Not many have been seasoned for the hard command in crisis management. I give the nod to Giuliani for his handling of the aftermath of 9/11. But I find it difficult to wrap my mind around their partisan rigidity. A militancy to party, not country.

Mario Cuomo, analyzing the presidential campaign said, "It will be about charisma, money, and lots of bulls_ _t. Vision, substance, and specifics will be hard to find." This reinforces the growing public perception of their dislike and distrust of politics and politicians. It is early for desperation but listen to some gems: Hillary turning into Harriet Tubman; Obama's dissertation on violence; McCain's hip-hop version of "Bomb, Bomb, Bomb, Iran;" Edwards' $400 haircut. They are becoming victims of their own poor judgment and fodder for the press.

We have paid dearly for the ineptitude of a bad run of recent presidents. Some, because of their timidity, led us down that dusty road, into that gulley of indecisiveness, where you lose control of the outcome and diminish your legacy.

David Halberstram, responding to what he felt was the one central question about Vietnam said, "How so many smart people could have been tragically wrong." He could have been talking about today.

Danger surrounds us, and multi threats to our security abound. This is no time for a wobbly and wired-for-weakness commander-in-chief. As I study the candidates, I can't help but wonder how many smart people in this country will make a dumb choice on the next president. Again.

A PROGRESS REPORT FOR THE PRESIDENT

Our past presidential election was unpredictable and historic. Hillary Clinton was shoo-in, but no one has adequately explained how she missed the turn to the White House. The president knows she still poses a threat to his future so he has reduced her to irrelevancy.

So let's update the progress and performance of our newly elected president. His eloquence has exuded a confidence that outstrips its validity. The gift of persuasive speech makes one fall prey to the ever-present seduction of narcissism. He is beginning to sound like an oracle. Instead of redeeming proclamations, we hear scolding admonitions (Bush left us a helluva mess).

It began in his inaugural address: "On this day we gather because we have chosen hope over fear, unity of purpose over conflict and discord." Yet discord has been the theme of his time in office.

He began to fill his quiver with the cop and Harvard professor "two-step." Branched out to the Arizona illegal immigration "nose-poke." And tops it with the mosque building at ground zero by volunteering to lead a sing-song of Kumbaya.

We have a nation crying out to him to fix the border. Isn't a bad economy enough to bear without waiting for the hammer to drop on healthcare reform? Our national debt has never seen the foreboding darkness of a trillion-dollar bottomless pit. And constantly the din of partisan insurgency. Since numbers are our sole standard of success, the General Quarters (Navy call to battle stations) has just sounded.

Problem solving needs the application of wisdom. Persuasive narrative, single-minded intent, guided by intrepid resolve and steadfast spirit. Qualities tempered by time in the trenches. Clint "Dirty Harry" Eastwood gives rise to the diminishing development of real national leadership when he says, "The guys who won World War II and that whole generation have disappeared and now we have a bunch of teen-age twits." Just how did so many wend their way into the hallowed halls of our nation's capital?

RETURN TO CHILDHOOD

It is professed that we all experience two childhoods: when we are born, and when we become very elderly. I see where retired Cardinal Edward Egan has entered that second stage by proclaiming his innocence of any involvement in the cover-up of sexual abuse as Bishop of Bridgeport (Advocate, 2/7/12). Similar allegations followed his predecessor Bishop Curtis, and his replacement Bishop Lori. Apparently too deep in prayer, Bishop Lori failed to notice Fr. Jude Fay would rob his parish, St. John's, Noroton, of over a million dollars during his many years as pastor. As an added benefit, he conveniently carried on a homosexual relationship right in the rectory. But the doozy was Bishop Lori paying an elite law firm over one million dollars to suppress public disclosure of payouts to sexual abuse victims. The case was carried all the way to the Supreme Court where it was rejected.

All three bishops, paralyzed by spiritual cowardice, could not perceive a remedy, so they resorted to cover-up. The accompanying tragedy was their failure of accountability to their "good priests," which would also put them under suspicion. Great institutions define themselves by remaining free of scandal.

Bishops are the successors to the Apostles, the original twelve chosen by Christ to spread the Gospel after he floated back home. They were penniless, lacked transportation and shelter, and relied on others for sustenance. Their mission was to evangelize. Their reward? Martyrdom. Today's Bishops are of superior intellect, sophisticated, and live high. Their mission? Raise funds. Their reward? Obeisance and luxury.

In her book, "Catholics at a Crossroads: Cover-up, Crisis, and Cure," Eileen P. Flynn, Professor at St. Peter's College, writes, "Raymond Schroth, S.J. (a professor at that college and a newspaper columnist) suggests that bishops should attend a 'penance service in Yankee Stadium.'" There the bishops should toss their embroidered vestments, mitres, and crosiers into a bonfire, replace them with sack cloth and a walking stick, and go forth to preach the good news. And become more accessible to their flock without the requisite of bearing gifts, or bending a knee. I agree. Do you?

ENOUGH MONUMENTS FOR BAD RESUMES

Chris Dodd, Charles Rangel, and Ted Kennedy come to mind when I am reminded our Founding Fathers forged honest government as our rightful heritage. We all determine our course. Unfortunately, we are remembered for our tracks we leave in the mud. Chris Dodd for bad mortgages. Charles Rangel for dodging taxes, Ted Kennedy for Chappaquiddick. When Dodd gave his farewell speech to Congress, he was carried away on the shoulders of his colleagues as if he were a coach who just won the big game. Rangel cried his way thru censure, which was a silly-putty punishment. And Ted was hailed as the watchdog against Republican largesse.

Bill Ayers, a close friend and advisor to President Obama, along with Bernadine Dohrn, flirted with anarchy. "We didn't plant enough bombs," they still claim. They came closer to bringing this country down than the war that precipitated their violence. In the 60's, they both were part of that revolutionary event that destabilized the structures of certainty that shaped our lives and our culture, and rent the fabric of the primacy of civility.

Why do we continue to build monuments to our public servants with bad resumes? When we were kids and got caught with our hands in the cookie jar, we were led to the woodshed. After telling a fib, my father put his arm around my shoulder and said, "Life is so much simpler when you tell the truth. If you keep hugging a lie, you will never be free." He taught me the ultimate wisdom that truth is absolute. We all grew up with this familial adage: Mothers know best. Sometimes fathers know, too.

TRAYVON MARTIN TRAGEDY

The recent tragedy of Trayvon Martin is being mishandled by Florida authorities allowing Al Sharpton and Jesse Jackson to rush to the site as saviors in waiting. A scene they have repeated many times, while noble in intent, has become Orwellian in purpose. Law and judgment is required here, but it is absent. Sharpton and Jackson bear the title of Reverend. But it smothers their history, corposant by title but hard-scrabble by deed. Sharpton would trap himself in the Tawana Brawley scandal, while Jackson could not keep his sexual hi-jinks secret. They both ingratiate themselves as the voice of black America, but sully their worthiness as successors to Martin Luther King. I see two angry men who arouse an angry fellowship not as a virtue, but as showtime for recycled verbiage. Even Spike Lee, the renowned N.Y. Knicks cheerleader, joins them waving his pom-poms. All three reduce to rubble the right to assemble, because they make it inflammatory.

Relevant today is the quandary of our racial history. A newly founded nation imported slavery to assist its growing agriculture, especially cotton in the South. It has become an indelible scourge that remains still. The Civil War would be fought to eliminate this human vassalage. Fellow Americans would kill each other (close to a half million) sometimes brother against brother. President Lincoln would provide the leadership to preserve the Union. Can you imagine the consequences if the South had won?

When the war ended, Lincoln would legislate amnesty for all former slaves. He proposed each would be granted forty acres and a mule. This would allow them to become independent entrepreneurs, which would lead to assimilation, and opportunities to economic and national political leadership. But his assassination would allow the South to smudge this remediation for over fifty years. And few rise to self-serving emissaries such as Sharpton and Jackson, masters of inaccurate articulation that fosters division over unity.

COMMENTS ON A GOOD PRIEST

In a Letter to the Editor (2/12/08), Joseph Gross takes the Advocate to task for its editorial (2/6/08) citing Fr. Michael Moynihan's de-frocking for financial mismanagement and cohabitating with his former music director. Mr. Gross praises Fr. Moynihan as a "good priest" for his "Christian caring work" as chaplain to cadets at the New York Maritime College which he attended.

Bishop Law of Boston, and Fr. Jude Fay of St. John's, Noroton, were also called "good priests," now mired in scandal, forced to resign, and one going to prison. Before their fall, they gave great Sunday sermons, conducted spiritual enhancing retreats, and charmed their parishioners with warm and glowing personalities. This is the veil they hide behind. The charm and seduction that masks their dark side. But deception brings them down.

What is soul-searing to me, is the number of parishioners who laud and praise all three for their "good works" but ignore their proven betrayal of their church and the church community. Being a so-called "good priest" does not mitigate the evil and harm they do.

Jesus warned us how convincing His false imitators can be. He railed against the unscrupulous priests of His time (Pharisees, Sadducees). When they tried to trap Him with seditious questions, (Whose commands should we obey, Your's or Caesar's?), He called them hypocrites and Whited Sepulchers full of dead men's bones.

Frauds and imposters are very adept at attracting the faithful to follow them into their fantasy world, until the deception disintegrates into painful disappointment. We are all subject to our passions, but misguided loyalty to wayward priests is not redemptive. Listen to what St. Paul has to say, "As I have said before, and now say again, if anyone preaches you a Gospel other than the one that you received, let that one be accursed."

LET ME ANSWER THE MONSIGNOR

I find the letter of Monsignor Frank Wissel (2/20/08) defending Father Michael Moynihan, a cohabitating, swindling, defrocked priest, devoid of logic and learning, sentient instruments one deploys in a tireless search for truth, justice, and wisdom. It is neither spiritually principled nor practical in application. He lauds the miscreant, then gets angry when victimized parishioners do not become a warmly receptive audience, but revert to "angry letter writing." This letter begs to be challenged.

Some emphatic points he makes must be engaged. He writes, "I have admired the faith and fidelity the diocese placed in Father Moynihan for he must've served it well." Can you wrap your mind around that? This is what sets-off angry letter writers, including myself. Where is the faith in this sordidness? Where is the fidelity in raping the parish treasury? This dizzying spiritual acuity is very, very, troubling. He goes on about "dedicated Catholics who criticize the diocese," and asks, "do they want to run the church **their** way?" Monsignor, this is **their** church, and they want it run the **right** way. The way Jesus directed it to be run.

He further states, "God cries everyday because of all the pain in the world." (Presumably caused by angry letter writers.) I say yes, he does. But he cries hardest over the pain caused by priests for vow-breaking homosexuality, who treat parish funds as their own, and those who cover and praise them.

He finally engages in spiritual gymnastics, asking all of us to pray, so that Father Moynihan can find healing and inner peace. There is something wrong here. Is it not the victimized parishioners who most need these graces? When church leaders are weak in serving their God, they end up serving themselves.

REJUVENATION OF HILLARY

Truth be known, Hillary Clinton was a certain choice to become the 44th President of the United States, and the first woman to be elected to that high office. But for some strange reason, which we will never know, she was thrown to the curb by the real power brokers that run this country behind the scenes. They chose Barack Obama, setting a precedent, as the first black president. A strange choice because he was a product of Chicago back-room politics, formulated by scandal-ridden former mayor Richard Daley. He now dangles as a puppet as the power brokers maneuver his strings.

We have seen this replay in the academic shortcomings of the Bush's, whose real achievements have been clearing brush at their Texas ranches. Because of Hillary Clinton's amnesia to her husband Bill's Lewinsky erotica, I swore to negate her political future. But vicissitudes change and I now join the stirring crowd calling in favor of her future run for the office she was denied. N.Y. Post columnist Linda Stasi and Joanna Molloy of the N.Y. Daily News are also touting encouragement for her to run alongside her husband Bill. But he has suddenly changed horses and now touts re-election for President Obama. Makes me wonder what he adds to his morning coffee. Perhaps he is shelving Hillary for four years defying logic that senility increases with passing years. Ronald Reagan was our fist octogenarian president. Are we headed to become the "Rocking Chair White House?"

A CHURCH IN CRISIS . . . STILL

There are similarities in the homosexual liaisons and pilfering of church treasuries in the cases of Father Jude Fay, St. John's, Noroton, and Father Michael Moynihan, St. Michael's, Greenwich. Father Fay would die of cancer before he could serve his prison sentence. Father Moynihan is not so lucky, as he starts his 5 months in prison (Stamford Advocate, 7/24/12). Both would steal over one million dollars.

In a 2/20/08 letter to the Advocate, Monsignor Frank Wissel, St. Mary's, Greenwich, would defend Father Moynihan and chastise parishioners for condemning his thievery. In response to Father Wissel, I, too, would like to take the Monsignior to task for his misguided defense of a cohabitating, swindling, defrocked priest. What stands out in Father Wissel's letter is this: "God cries every day because of all the pain in the world," (presumably caused by angry letter writers). I say, yes, He does. But He cries hardest for vow-breaking homosexuality, those who treat parish funds as their own, and those who cover and praise them.

Both of these cases occurred under the diademical watchfulness of Bishop Lori. Such astute vigilance gained him the promotion of Archbishop of Baltimore. Spending one million dollars on legal fees to keep payments to children abused by his pedophile priests from publication, had to enhance his promotion. How many treasuries will be emptied in Baltimore to gain his red hat? Then, join former Bishop Law of Boston who was run out of town only to be promoted in Rome, as the Curia sang, "How Many Miles to Babylon."

Do you know where all this crumbling started? With the onset of Vatican II when many good priests and nuns left the church for the promises of secular life that proved to be illusional. When all reverence disintegrated as the Latin Mass was replaced by the vernacular. It also fostered the idea among bad priests that remained that they could get away with predatory behavior. And they did, because bishops turned a blind eye, or did not know how, or want to correct it. Jesus foresaw the deviancy that would infiltrate His growing church. You will find it in one of His most remarkable sayings, "When the Son of Man comes, will He find faith left on Earth?"

OBAMA'S TRUE CHARACTER COMES OUT IN SCANDAL

The mother of all political hustles was Bill Clinton's: "It depends on what the meaning of *is* is."

News coming out of Chicago might top it.

Governor Rod Blagojevich is neck-deep in the scandal of a Senate seat for sale. Wire taps disclose that tentacles reach out to President-elect Barack Obama, and his newly appointed chief of staff, Rahm Emanuel. It seems the ghost of former Mayor Richard Daley, who put the diadem on political corruption, still hangs over that "toddling town" like the ghost of Marley haunting Scrooge.

Obama's release of his "internal" probe (he immediately fled to Hawaii to escape the heat) absolving his aides of any "inappropriate" contact with the governor, is like confessing to yourself and receiving self-subscribed absolution.

The warning signs were there early in Obama's campaign (the Rev. Jeremiah Wright, Tony Rezko, Bill Ayers), were winked away by an accommodating press and a fawning following, which failed to ask the hard questions.

The philosophy of the noble ancient Greeks is steeped in the requirement for political leadership: competence and character. What stone do I uncover to find these qualities in our nation's capital? Political corruption is not a freak flaw. Nor is it an anomaly in our social fabric.

A recent photo-op shows Obama and Emanuel with the beleaguered governor in a tight circle. A band of brothers, all smiles and palsy-walsy, embarked on a "faith journey." But after the oil spill, the trustworthy covenant members cut the governor adrift, and scurried to seek River Jordan cleansing. Caught with his hand in the cookie jar, Mr. Blagojevich, full of spunk, stands boldly before the cameras. No one is this brazen unless he has some markers to call in.

I have to admit: Barack Obama's election was a sunny story. He sold us on being a president of change and hope and a new America. But his call to arms is becoming a pious generality that keeps chinking and changing.

WHEN STEWARDS BECOME VANDALS

The authors of the Constitution left us a message that political service is for the good of all and in union with the will of the people. Where has this stewardship gone? Here are some examples where the stewards became vandals: Charles Rangel, Tom Daschele, Tim Geithner, Nancy Killefer, all exposed as tax cheats. Chris Dodd abrogates his oversight responsibility as chairman of the Banking Committee by availing himself of subprime mortgages that ignited our financial collapse. These are blistering displays of parasitic ironies. Facades of political purity who grub for advantage. By repeated re-election they give themselves an immunity to navigate the darkness. When exposed, the brethren adjourn to the Capitol lounge, and over cocktails out-snicker each other, equating themselves to schoolchildren getting caught tossing spitballs in the classroom.

There was a time when we as a nation stood fully confident in the worthiness of our causes. Our leaders were dedicated servants of the public. They had national appeal—grace, trust, quiet courage—to muster the productive enterprise to contribute to the common good. Just name one upon whom we can pin a star, as I want to stand up and cheer.

Where are the venerable watchdogs who use the measure of law to keep order and everyone on an acceptable plateau of virtue? The ugly reality is the depth and magnitude of wrongdoing in high office is being tolerated with a wink and a shrug.

Insider politics, like insider trading, ordains the rot that bleeds across our headlines and TV screens. The latest shooting stars? Bernard Madoff and Governor Blagojevich. Both would lead us to the fountain, but it is like drinking from a fire hose.

There is a noticeable absence of high regard for our elected officials. Public explanations of their wrongdoing are effusive bromides that become a crisis of the truth. It starts when they mistake the mud of the Potomac for the Rubicon, then stretch the boundaries of their limits, and never find their way back.

Harry Truman, after his first day in the Senate, said, "What am I doing here?" A year later he said, "What are they doing here?"

Times were hard when I was young. After a long day of complaining, my father took me to the local pub and said, "Everything looks rosy after a few stiff drinks." Thanks Pop.

PUTTING BULLIES ON THE RUN

Leadership is defined as taking command in the crucible of the moment. Bullying is that crucible that motivated President Obama to call a national conference at the White House to examine the issue and to seek resolutions. George Jepsen, recently elected Ct. Attorney General, is proposing legislation to make cyber-bullying a crime. Kind of late, aren't you fellas? Where were you when the body count was rising?

School bullying has gone unchallenged for so long that it has become expansive and deadly, leading to suicides of many of our children. All the way back to my high school days (1939-1943), which I will detail.

I had expected the president to be forceful and decisive. Issuing a command to all bullies to halt their fear-inducing threats or the consequences will be swift and compelling. Instead he was full of mushy lamentations (bullying is not a rite of passage). It frightened the bullies into shake-and-bake chuckles.

I wrote in this newspaper (Op. Ed. 5/5/10) how determined neighborhood kids had the resiliency and courage to solve a schoolyard problem a White House conference now struggles with. Of my experience with a bully 70 years ago, and how he was cured because we brought the hammer down. Not as a taste of revenge (although it was entertained), but as a desire to be free of his nemesis. My eldest son, 35 years later, would emulate our method to tame a bully who menaced his kid sister right here in one of our local schools. It had ramifications, but better bold than fearful.

You see, you do not talk a bully down, no more than you can talk a cat down from a tree. The bully must be made to feel the sting he administers. I know this remedy was not proposed at the White House conference. It should have because it works. This is not a mock, but how soon do we read about the next suicide? I guarantee it will not be my first grade grandson. He is being instructed how to tame the tempest. Call me a dinosaur, but don't question its effectiveness.

WHY DEFEND A PRODIGAL PRIEST?

I find it troublesome and soul-searing that Monsignor Frank Wissel, a respected, witty and loveable priest, would go to such lengths (Stamford Advocate 2/20/08) to defend a prodigal priest. Like Father Jude Faye of St. John's, Noroton, who is going to prison, Father Michael Moynihan is de-frocked by Bishop Lori for the same offenses (vow-breaking homosexuality and financial shenanigans).

The Monsignor's melodramatic defense of a fallen priest is spiritual effluvium. The church is in crisis and his letter adds to its tragic failures. What gauge is he using as he praises Father Moynihan for his abundance of "Faith and Fidelity?" Where is the Faith in committing sodomy in the rectory? Where is the Fidelity in raping the parish treasury? I would love to borrow the prism the good monsignor uses to view this sordidness as salvific.

The "angry letter writers" he chastises, shows his letter does not pass the test of irenics, nor soothes his "righteous indignation."

It is charitable to pray for healing and inner peace for Father Moynihan, but in this case, is it not the victimized parishioners who are most in need of these graces? You cannot "slosh" your way to sainthood. I find when church leadership are weak in serving their God, they end up serving themselves.

FAULTY LOGIC

The jury has decreed the death penalty for Steven Hayes for his commission of a draconian crime against the Petit family. Rape, torture, murder by fire. We the People nod in agreement. But the newspaper's editorial board, "Death penalty compromises our humanity" (Stamford Advocate, 11/9/10) says not so fast. We have no right to kill the killer.

This brings me to a momentary pause for reflection. This faulty logic and skimpy reasoning titillates my inner stirrings and visceral undulations. You see, it is not so much we are taking the life of Hayes, but he has forfeited his right to it. The gavel of jurisprudence says so.

The commandment, "Thou shall not kill," infers in an unlawful way. But leaves open the question of a lawful way.

Scripture does not restrict or forbid it. St. Thomas Aquinas writes that by rule of law, society has the right to protect itself by putting to death individuals who, through their heinous crimes, become a further threat to the innocent. In Matthew 18:10, where Jesus delineates the virtue of childhood, He goes on to say, "but were a man to be an occasion to fall of any of these little ones who believe in Me, it would be better for him to have a stone from a donkey-mill tied to his neck and drowned in the open sea."

The editorial says, "We as a society must operate on a moral plain high above that of our most depraved members." God says you are wrong. Take your challenge to Him.

By man's law, the crime of Steven Hayes leads to the grave. In Mark 9:48, God's law takes you beyond. To Gehenna, "where the fire is unquenchable, and the worm never dies." I will bet you my golden tresses (I had them in my youth) that the verdict for an unspeakable crime, unless changed by a national referendum, will still put you on the road to Hades. Nice try.

COW SENSE

Spurred by Al Gore's book, "An Inconvenient Truth," climatology is becoming a new religion. For ecological mandarins, global warming is becoming a greater threat than radical Islam. They are especially obsessed with the effects of cow flatulence on climate. They claim unless we control the passing of gas by our cows, the polar ice cap will melt.

The cattle ranchers are being besieged to take immediate curative action. But nobody is offering any preventive measures. This is not like curbing smoking. How do you inhibit a cow from performing his natural digestive process?

The climatologists are offering this suggestion: that ranchers herd their cows into specially constructed sheds to capture the gas they emit (methane) in special containers where it will be used to generate electricity. Impractical, implausible, and overly expensive, say the ranchers. It changes their industry from beef production to vapor chasers and emission canners.

Like the protection conferred on the snail darter that impeded flood control projects, the watchdog environmentalists threaten the extinction of our steaks, our briskets, our prime rib, our roasts, our stews, and our burgers. It reminds me of the pseudo advocacy of vegetarians: "Exactly nine white raisins, soaked in gin and allowed to dry, should be eaten every day to alleviate the crippling pains of arthritis."

WHY PHONIES CRY WHEN CAUGHT

Chris Elsberry, in his article, "Calhoun's Image Takes a Big Hit" (Stamford Advocate 2/23/11), defines how the wheels have come off college basketball, especially at U-Conn. Jeff Jacobs (Hartford Courant) likens Calhoun to playing Sgt. Schultz in that old TV comedy, Hogan's Heroes, "I know nothing." He calls it pathetically laughable as it is profoundly troubling. The coach has fallen into that recruiting pit, where who cares if a player can't spell CAT and beats up his girlfriends, but sure can play basketball.

Apparently, winning a couple of national championships, and being elected to the Hall of Fame, you acquire a bulletproof mantra. You can wade in the sewer and come out smelling like roses. Surprisingly, many alumni and ardent supporters wink away these indiscretions. Whoop-de-damn-do coach, we got your back. Everybody is doing it, so we have to keep up. Just bring us a championship.

Professing to consult his lawyer to regain his halo, he seeks to find joy in his jadedness. While his apologists don misguided robes of piety, because his championship trophies have turned into baubles that sully the academic integrity of our great university. Perhaps he should attend one of Geno's clinics to get it right.

REQUIEM FOR THE YMCA

A recent meeting (7/16/07) called by the Board of Directors to inform the membership of their decision to sell and close the YMCA was stormy and vexing. Those of us in attendance were unprepared for the finality of the pending sale, and the short notice to vacate by October 31. We all wished it could have been handled differently with a better result.

We were told the YMCA has turned into an unredeemable liability (financially and structurally). Many factors were cited (proliferation of private fitness centers, loss of memberships, aging structure). This did not happen overnight. It was slow and accumulative. It was the consensus of those of us in attendance, that when the cracks began to show, the political, corporate, and business leadership, as well as the membership, should have been called upon to remedy the situation. Funds could have been raised to restore financial stability, structural integrity, and remain at the existing site.

The community would have risen to keep the Y viable. Nobody wants to see the death of the YMCA. This loss is deleterious to the city, and it wounds all human service organizations. The funds needed earlier would be much, much less than what will be needed to build new.

We were told when the building is demolished and the membership dispersed, there would be a rebirth. The Phoenix would rise from the ashes. It sounded more like a requiem. What is also being lost is the prime downtown location, where a recent survey showed the membership desired to stay.

A recent editorial (7/19/07) in the Advocate outlined the uncertain future the YMCA faces. Better planning (site procurement, architectural rendition of the new facility, cost estimates, fund-raising leadership) should be in place before the building is sold. It questioned the urgency.

Tom Sanseverino, President of the Board of Directors, and Susan Dinnocenti, Acting Executive Director, are honorable and well-meaning individuals. They face a monumental task in relocating and building a new YMCA. Many YMCA alumni still reside in the city, united in a common bond of their life-transforming membership experience. What stays with us most is the sacred trust inherent in the mission of the YMCA. Along with the existing members, closing the door on our second home feels like a loss in the family. This loss becomes personal, and it hurts.

Mr. Gawlak is the retired Director of Fitness of the Stamford YMCA, Serving from 1955-1986; he is a lifetime member, and a regular participant.

ADVOCATE WRONG AGAIN

I recently challenged the editorial board of this newspaper concerning capital punishment. I now accept the new gauntlet. The Advocate editorializes, "According to a Pentagon report, the vast majority of active-duty troops see no difficulty in ending "Don't ask, don't tell." This is smurf. The truth is, cites Cal Thomas, noted syndicated columnist, "If the policy is reversed, tens of thousands of those currently in service will retire or quit." And Sen. John McCain says, "Repealing the ban could create an "alarming" troop retention problem when the military is short-handed." Secretary of Defense Robert Gates said, "Congress had better act before the law is imposed by judicial fiat." A National Review Online editorial labeled Gates' comment "blackmail via judicial imperialism." This is major lobbying by the President, Secretary of Defense, and Joint Chiefs Chairman. They need to be reminded that the Constitution defines and limits their powers. That the polemical assumption that abnormality is morally neutral is harmful.

Recently, a Rutgers University student committed suicide by jumping off the George Washington Bridge. He was distraught over the Internet posting of a secretly filmed sexual encounter he had with another male. ABC News anchor Diane Sawyer called this event, "a romantic encounter." This is another synecdoche of the moral sepsis into which our country has sunk since the 1960's. A time when the cream of our youth stormed off our campuses, untamed and undisciplined, engaging in drug-crazed orgies. Public wantonness by children of privilege, which cowed their parents into becoming accessories. It became a disheartening revolutionary event that destabilized the structures of certainty that shaped our culture and our lives. The residue remains with us today. Some in our top leadership in Washington.

Do you know the last region of lotus and locusts, whose preamble also was "Don't ask, don't tell," was reduced to dust and ashes by a rain of hellfire and brimstone? You see, the prince of

Darkness is not Cupid, nor does love flourish in his domain. Dante defines this very clearly.

We are a nation of majority rule. And the majority is telling the don't ask, don't tell-ers, who thirst for military service, to join the French Foreign Legion

ECHOES OF LAPTOPS AT UCONN

I have always believed that the University of Connecticut was an academic institution, and not the Department of Corrections. But a recent story in the Hartford Courant (12/16/07) about basketball recruit Nate Miles stated, "Oft maligned teen may soon be in Storrs," challenges that assumption. Coach Calhoun considering a scholarship offer to this troubled youth with a long-troubled past just lit up warning signs. Remember the stolen laptops, and the coach's Twinkie resolution of layered hypocrisy and starchy morality on "not abandoning kids who get into trouble," especially if they are your ticket to a championship?

Reclamation projects are noble and commendable. But when that reclamation leads to a degree of tolerance for everything that is producing an unwillingness to restrict anything, then it is time to draw the line.

Follow-the-bouncing-ball is not an approved remedial intervention for unacceptable behavior, and a university that provides sanction crosses that threshold where it mortgages its soul for a piece of net. The coach is about to go there again. And he is allowed, because college athletics, like hogs, have been gorging at the money trough too long; that gate receipts trump academic integrity.

It doesn't have to be this way. Great universities are defined by how free they remain from scandal, especially in their athletic departments. Renowned university presidents demand this mandate. Myles Brand of Indiana fired basketball coach Bob Knight for habitual misconduct. Nancy Zimpher of Cincinnati did the same to coach Bob Huggins. Queasy ones at UConn expire in their silence and wet their pants.

FEAST OR FAMINE

Much is being said and done today to reduce obesity in our country, especially in children. But the recent passing of John Kenneth Galbraith reminds me of what he wrote in his novel, "The Affluent Society" (1958), "more die in the United States of too much food than of too little."

I was a young lad growing up during the Great Depression, which was a time of "too little." Because of the economic hardships of that time, there wasn't enough food for anyone to become obese. The homeless shelters and soup kitchens of today are minor league compared to the great depression of my time. The whole country was one big bread line and soup kitchen.

Albert Maltz defines the conditions of that time best in his book, "New Masses" (1932). He describes the protagonist walking the streets of New York, looking for work and a meal: "She was sitting on the stoop. When I walked by, she crossed her legs showing her thighs and winked. I walked over to her. 'How about it, Hon?' I said, "Christ, Kid, if I had any dough, I'd rather eat."

Those of us who have been in the trenches for 85 or more years can relate to both these extremes: 1930's (too little), and 1990's (too much). If it is all right with you, I'll choose the hefty side, thank you.

SINGING IN THE SHOWER

During idle chatter with friends, I sometimes ask for their recall of happy moments in their life. What momentarily lifts their spirit and set them free. Caught off guard, they pause, wander into deep thought, scrunch their brows, then relate various and sundry telling moments. Some frivolous, some thoughtful. But none recall "Singing In The Shower" as most liberating.

I am dating myself, but the refrains of, That Old Gang of Mine, By the Old Cider Mill, and Sweet Adeline, love stories of old and refined in their simplicity, while best for harmonizing, do well in solo. Customs and habits change. Today the shower room has become the place where lullabies come to die. The next time you dine out with friends, ask when they last sang in the shower.

POLITICAL MAGIC

There's nothing more disturbing than the organized joy of the jaded. A recent photo (July 22), featuring President Obama heaping plaudits upon Barney Frank and Chris Dodd, adds validity to that circular argument that reverses connivance unto congratulations.

This occasion of high praise is intended to mask their engendered financial collapse as award-winning financial reform.

Being co-chairs of Banking Committee, these two stalwarts precipitated the crash of Wall Street and near collapse of our nation's economy through their sub-prime mortgage gerrymander, that still has the banking industry sinking in an unprecedented number of foreclosures.

It has as its equivalent two bank robbers returning the money they stole and expecting a reward.

There have been many capers by our moral re-doubtable legislators devising cutesy, authentic means of reclaiming their reputations. This steals the prize from former Sen. Wilbur Mills being fished out of the tidal basin after a drunken romp with one of his chickadees, Fannie Fox.

Change in tides occurs every 12 hours. In politics, it occurs when their tails catch fire (note Charles Rangel). It reminds me of a sermon I once heard. The presiding minister extolling the evil of alcohol proclaimed, "If I had all the whiskey in the world, I'd take it and pour it into the river." Sermon complete, he sat down. The song leader stood very cautiously, and announced with a smile, "For our concluding song, let us sing Hymn #365: 'Shall We Gather at the River'."

A WAR TOO LONG

Our country has a long history of war. I was the youngest of five
brothers that fought in World War II. All wars are different, but the
trenches never change. That history continues as we are engaged
in war in distant lands of Iraq and Afghanistan. Knocking down
our twin towers on 9/11 is justification for our troops being in
Afghanistan. It is in response to that enormous evil perpetrated by
Osama Bin Laden. The invasion of Iraq became questionable when
weapons of mass destruction proved to be a myth. And it took ten
years of fighting to bring measurable progress there. In Afghanistan
the surge (adding 30,000 more troops) is beginning to bring success.

There is an old saying, "When you lose a war, you fire the
general." After Pearl Harbor we not only fired a General (Walter
Short), but also an Admiral (Husband Kimmel). When the war in
Iraq started to go bad with rising casualties, the cry went up to fire a
president (George W. Bush). George Washington suffered his Iraqi
moment at Valley Forge. Can you imagine the consequences if he
was fired then? James Madison, after his ill-advised War if 1812,
convinced him the call to arms requires greater prudence. Under
great criticism, President Harry Truman fired General Douglas
MacArthur during the Korean War, for proposing a nuclear strike to
stem the surprise Chinese intervention at the Yalu River.

We all long for a "feel-good" ending for these wars. I want to
believe what president Bush said at Arlington at his last Memorial
Day address, "They know this war will end one day, as all wars
do. Our duty is to ensure that its outcome justifies the sacrifices
made by those who fought and died in it." This is now for the new
Commander-In-Chief to carry out.

Our Republic was born to break away from familial ascendancy of
monarchy. In our continuing experiment of government by self-rule,
keeping the presidency in the family has proven a bad precedent. A
father and son presidency has proven this. Had Hillary been elected
president, inheritance by family would have continued, with Chelsea
itching for her turn. This is not in the best interest of a nation crying
for new leadership. President Obama promised us change his clarion
call in his campaign. Will we know it when we see it?

PRIEST AND BISHOP ASK VICTIMS TO PAY

Father Jude Fay, asking parishioners of St. John's church of Noroton to help pay his legal fees for stealing $ 1.4 million from them (Advocate, 5/25) crosses the line of jurisprudence. The Bishop of Spokane, Wash. trumps him.

Bishop William Skylstad of the Diocese of Spokane, Wash. filed for Chapter 11 bankruptcy, and now needs $ 48 million to settle 177 claims of sexual abuse. He is asking his 82 parishes to donate $ 10 million to bail him out. The priest and the bishop re-define God's and man's law: victims pay the price for the criminal. This is spiritual extortion.

The real issue here is the spiritual bankruptcy of the many bishops who abetted the sexual abuse of children by priests under their watch, to burgeon themselves into this financial morass. Bishops who violated the fundamental principles of crisis management, became thieves of the sacred.

Some parish priests are using the parable of the Good Samaritan to convince the faithful to contribute to the bail-out fund: "The Good Samaritan was not at all responsible for the problem, but he was the one who took care of the problem." This constant plunder of verity leaves me dizzy. If Bishop Lori asked the parishioners of St. John's church in Noroton to replace the $ 1.4 million stolen by Father Jude Fay, under the pretext of the Good Samaritan, you would hear the roof blow off all the way to Oshkosh.

Bishop Skylstad himself is being accused of sexually abusing a woman when she was a student in the 60's. "I never broke my vow of chastity," he claims. He doesn't deny it, but invoking his chastity sets him free.

In conferring with learned people, deep into the study of church history and the evolution of the hierarchy, indicates it will take a generation before meaningful change abates the corruption. Meaning, the timeframe entrenched offenders get too old to rule, and we sweep away the wreckage of a dispirited church they leave behind.

Irreligious forces have their holiday in moments of great catastrophe. To expedite a quicker day of judgment, we need a profound Pontiff who will exercise the righteous anger of Jesus, and put the rope to the malefactors who desecrate His Father's House.

MONSIGNOR ADMONISHING CRITIC

Congratulations to D. Morgan Saunders on an excellent letter (3/3/08) bashing Monsignor Frank C. Wissel and his obnoxious letter telling us sinners to shut up about Father Michael Moynihan (2/20/08). While quite to the point, I would like to add the following:

I don't know Father Moynihan, but I'd bet that he's a nice guy, probably a wonderful guy who helps a lot of people. But he is only a part or a result of the issue; he is part of an organization that is out of touch and out of control.

So what if he lives with another guy; at least he's in a stable relationship. He probably shouldn't, however, be a priest, at least not under the rules he has chosen for himself.

If he wants to remain a priest, then he's got to do something about it, like fighting to change the rules. I know it's not easy, maybe not even possible in his lifetime; but instead of trying, he and his brother rule-breakers get into step and do as they are told by their dysfunctional organization. As a result, they live a life consumed with lies; they deceive those who believe in them.

I feel sorry for Father Moynihan. He does have some unpleasant issues to be addressed. I don't, however, feel sorry for Monsignor Wissel, mister holier-than-thou who feels that we can't understand or reason on our own, and that we somehow need him to show us the way.

The good monsignor tells us, "We are all sinners," and I'm sure most of us are. That aside, I want to point out to the monsignor that whether we are sinners or not, we didn't decide to become priests as did he and his fellow sinners (his words, not mine).

He then states that "it is not my purpose to discuss the innocence or guilt, sinfulness or goodness of my brother Michael Moynihan;" but then goes on to infer that we, his flock, should keep our thoughts and opinions to ourselves, since we are those "who really know nothing." In other words, he can say to us what he wants but we can't.

He goes on to admonish "Those who criticize the diocese—do they realize how hurtful this situation has been to every Catholic and non-Catholic who reads about this, to the employees of the diocese, to every priest?" Again, his implied solution is that what happens in the diocese stays in the diocese, so just shut up and put your money in the basket.

I know I'm not perfect, but for one, I'm sick of religious "leaders" who seek their positions, claim to know better than we, admonish us to be reverent, warn us to be like Jesus, tell us to keep our thoughts to ourselves, ask for our hard-earned donations in every way possibly imaginable; and then do as they please violate every tenet they are supposed to uphold, betray our trust, assume we are fools, and then lie to us.

Monsignor Wissel was right: he should have listened to his mother's advice to "keep his mouth shut and let people think you are a fool because if you open it you will remove all doubt."

CHURCH'S TASK

The message I would like to give to Monsignor Frank C. Wissel regarding his letter ("Critics of diocese should think before they give opinions," Greenwich Time, 2/22/08) is the following:

How dare you give us such a condescending lecture about this. My message to you, sir, is: "Get your house in order, *now!*"

For years upon years, the leaders of your church have turned a blind eye to those who do not follow Christ's example. I am tired of all the hypocrisy!

Turn all your energy, sir, to making sure your fellow priests follow Christ's example and do the right thing.

Enough with the lectures. Take care of the church's business, and go after your church leaders who allow these "rogue" so-called "men of God" to take advantage of others, and in many cases ruin young children's lives.

God's followers and their children are depending on you to follow Christ's example. Give us lectures on the Bible, not on defending the evil-doers.

May God have a special place for all those who harm our innocent children!

LOSS OF A UNIQUE FRIEND

My 5-year-old grandson Charlie was helping me clear the yard of branches caused by a recent wind storm. Out in the middle of the road was a squirrel apparently run over by a car. Upon close examination, it turned out to be the one-eyed squirrel I wrote about in the newspaper (July 19, 2004). I knew it was him by a distinctive identifying mark (a nick in his left ear).

He wasn't quick enough to outmaneuver the other squirrels and birds for the nuts I fed them. So he would come to the back porch and pitter-patter with his paws on the storm door. I also knew he was there by the low, guttural squawk of a scolding daw berating him.

As I gathered the remains for disposal, my grandson said, "Grandpa, he didn't look both ways." This was the cautionary admonition he was always given before crossing the street.

When you become attached to an animal (wild or pet), its death can rival the passing of a family member. We had to put down two pet cats because they became terminally ill with old age. As I took them to the veterinarian, I am still haunted by the sobs and tears of the children and grandchildren. I left it to my wife to do the consoling.

Pets are easily replaced. Just how do replace an adopted, lovable, one-eyed squirrel, who trundles sideways, has part of his ear missing, knocks on your door when hungry, and doesn't look both ways when crossing the street? Do you have a better children's fable?

The following is the letter Mr. Gawlak sent to the Advocate in July, 2004:

One-eyed squirrels?

It is time for a human interest story. With the passing of the fourth of July, it is time to set aside the political fireworks, as well.

I have become fond of a one-eyed squirrel who feeds on the acorns from my oak tree. He has a strange gait. He tilts his head to see from his one good eye, and trundles and stumbles sideways. The other squirrels seem to be aware of his handicap, and do not chase him away.

When the acorns are depleted, I toss out peanuts. He isn't fast enough to get his share, so he waddles to my side, tilts his head up to look at me, and I make sure he is fed. He keeps coming back until he has his fill (usually four or five will do).

Sometimes, he waits on my back porch. When he feels I'm too slow in responding, he pitter-patters on the storm door with his front paws.

When my wife has to go out, and I hear her scream, it is time for me to hide. She yells at me for traumatizing them both, as she almost steps on him. Because of this, when we shop at the market, I have standing orders: "No peanuts in the shopping cart."

Nobody ever said life is easy.

Let me conclude by making a comparison. There is ample evidence that the politicos who populate Hartford and Washington run the affairs of state and nation like that one-eyed squirrel: Stumbling and trundling and, at times, underfoot.

MILESTONES
AND
MEMORIES

SEVEN COUSINS

There were seven cousins
Who lived on a hill
They would get together on holidays
To feast and play and chill

Six were strong and tall
And one was very small
He came late, so he has to wait
To join the free-for-all

Four lived in New Milford
A growing country town
Where Michael and Nick could always be found
Driving their cars and trucks around

Over the ridge lived Jeff and Joe
Their house on a hill, where cows come and go
And when you come to visit, they could be found
Cutting the grass and tossing a ball around

In Huntington the other two lived
So far in the woods, you had to forgive
One Brian, the other Bill
Music was their game, and never got their fill

It was awhile but at last one came
He is the smallest, and Charles is his name
When he plays, it is with a vacuum
When he gets older, he will never touch one
Be sure to assume

We tried to give this picture a name
We tried and tried and came up lame
So let's unveil it for all to view
And the naming, we leave up to you

WINTERS OF OLD

Winters of today could never match the bitter, extended cold spells of days of my youth. The frost in the ground would be two feet thick. Snow would cover the ground from Thanksgiving to Easter. Zero-degree-weather would last for weeks. And the river would freeze a cover of ice three feet thick. Homes were heated by coal stoves. It was my chore to see enough coal and wood was stored by the stove in the kitchen. Bedrooms were not heated, but all beds had three-feet-thick quilts stuffed with duck and goose down. On windy nights, you were serenaded by rattling windows. We were warmed in the local playground clubhouse by a large wood-burning pot-belly stove. It closed at 8 p.m., so we would go to the nearby YMCA. The director knew we were not members but let us stay to keep warm. Coal and fuel barges supplied the cities from Saybrook to Hartford. When the river froze, a Coast Guard ice-breaker would keep the channel open so the fuel barges could navigate upstream. We would stand on the ice and almost touch the barges as they moved by.

In Spring, we would bet on what day the ice would break and open the river. Chunks of ice would drift downstream for months. Spring brought heavy rains; and the river would turn muddy, rise to flood stage, and run heavy and fast, carrying debris and uprooted trees that were a danger if you ventured out there. By April and May, Shad and Alewives started their spawning runs upstream. Commercial fishermen, using hauling seines, would net them and sell them to fish markets, especially in New York City. Carp would also spawn at that time. They would fill the low-lying meadows that were flooded, but remained trapped when the waters receded. We would spear them and sell them to the local Jewish fish markets. Some of the Carp weighed 35 pounds, and the sale furnished us with spending money for candy, ice cream, and the movies.

A mile south of the city was a hill called "Duck Hill." After a heavy snow, we would sled and toboggan down that hill that provided a speedy and exhilarating run. Some storms would leave a glaze of ice an inch thick on the snow's surface. It increased the speed of your sled, but sometimes the sled's runners would break thru the ice layer and send you crashing, cutting and gashing your face.

The river supplied a source of recreation, adventure, and spending money; and I still go back there to fish with old boyhood friends to reminisce and feel young again.

1936 FLOOD—1938 HURRICANE

It was during the Great Depression that I would experience two of the greatest natural disasters to strike my hometown, Middletown, CT. Living on the banks of the Connecticut River would add to those catastrophes. The 1936 flood would rise to a level that I believe the Indians never saw. A plaque indicating the high water mark is located on the retaining wall leading to downtown. In the spring, with the melting snows up north, the river would rise near flood stage and was called the spring freshet. Three days of heavy rain, on top of the high water, would cause the greatest flood in history. We would raise chickens, ducks, and geese to add to the food supply for the dinner table. The river rose so rapidly, it drowned all the chickens. The ducks and geese swam away and were never seen again. By morning, the house was surrounded by water. We were evacuated, and I was housed at the Salvation Army for five days, and fed at the Armory Hall. When the waters receded, we were allowed to go home, as we lived upstairs in a two-family house. Silt was deposited everywhere, and had to be hosed by the Fire Department back into the receding river. The highway bridge that spanned the river was so damaged it had to be replaced. Many houses were swept away. Huge fuel oil storage tanks were dislodged and damaged, and were cut apart by acetylene torches and carted away, making that flood the most disastrous in our history.

Two years later (1938), we would be hit by the most damaging hurricane ever. There was no warning. The wind started to pick-up, and the rain grew heavier. At its peak, our house would shake. Looking out the window, I would see the chimney and part of the roof of the house across the street get blown away. All sorts of loose objects would be seen crashing by. My Mother, being an ardent devout Polish Catholic, would light candles and lead us in prayer. Is that what saved us? By morning, the worst was over. Going outside, the devastation was indescribable. The street our school was on had been lined with stately elms. Everyone was uprooted and made a maze and obstacle course we had to traverse. There were no power saws, and they had to clear by two-man saws. It took a year to cut them away, and another year to clear the stumps. Power lines were not extensive then, and power was restored in ten days. The city dump was an open dumping ground near the river. All the hurricane debris and tree trunks filled it in. It was then covered with soil and grass planted and became a playground. The heavy rain would cause the river to rise, but not as extensive as the 1936 flood. In ensuing years, there would be other hurricanes and floods, but none could match the devastation of 1936 and 1938.

FATHER MADDEN DEMONIZED

There is an old Mexican proverb that says: 'the truth should not offend." But twisting the truth does. And there has been a lot of "twisting" by Bishop Lori and Msgr. Wissel in his long and self-liberating letter. Let us examine some points.

When asked about hiring a private investigator, Fr. Madden is turned into the culprit, not the thieving priest (Fr. Fay) who stole 1.4 million dollars of parish funds. The crook gets a free pass to enjoy the fruits of his crime.

Bishop Lori offered Fr. Madden a leave of absence. Don't believe it. It was an order of raw ecclesiastical power. He was sent to "Siberia" to pray and do penance.

The Bishop took immediate steps to investigate. The horse had already left the barn, so he had to close the door.

In life, we all experience disappointments, some quite severe. The Msgr. is right. We all have to take a lot of punches. But the Bishop, forcing Fr. Madden to sign a letter of apology, was a "sucker punch." A punch so unwarranted it mutilated his spirit and crushed his vocation. "Something inside of me died when I was forced to sign that letter," said Fr. Madden in his letter of resignation.

"Fr. Madden needs to grow up, and act like a man." I agree. Fr. Madden should have told the Bishop where to go. Now, that would have been manly.

There are two sides to every story. That's right. All we have here is the Msgr.'s side. And it is all blame: Fr. Madden's immaturity; the spin of the press; refusal of the Msgr.'s counsel and safe haven; and abandoning God's gift. The Msgr. would have you believe Fr. Madden left the Priesthood ("picked up his marbles and went home because of some disappointment"). The truth is he was given a hefty shove by the Bishop. If this is a letter of love for Fr. Madden, a call to reconciliation, I fear for the rhetoric if he was disliked.

CONVENTION CLAMOR

The central dynamic of politics is connivance. The recent political conventions are proof. They are like tribal gatherings. When President Obama shouted, "More time needed," the hall erupted and the walls shook. When former President Bill Clinton said, "One million jobs are just around the corner," the unemployed broke ranks and headed for the nearest company door. Tears filled our eyes when Michelle Obama told us how family-loving her husband was. Re-elect us and the good times will roll. Sorry, Mr. President, the country is up to its neck in a trillion dollar pit of quicksand. Your musical rhetoric has stopped, and your tune is in discord. A week before, Clint "Dirty Harry" Eastwood would tell them all, "You did a lousy job, now get out."

President Obama, a gifted orator, and born for the podium, has proven to be poor behind the desk to run the country. He has proven that politics is an illusion of service which cloaks the corruption of power. George Will, noted columnist, writes, "Americans want from government not such flights of fancy, but sobriety; not fantasies about a world without scarcities and therefore without choices among our desires and appetites, but a mature understanding of the limits to government's proper scope and actual competence."

George Washington, our first president, transformed the prevailing form of government from a monarchy to experimental democracy. After his second term, he was so agitated by a growing oppositional aristocracy, he refused to run again. Today's aristocracy are the titans of finance and corporate moguls who have proven the misuse of power and wealth are the main sources of corruption. Where is that president who can guide our country by the way of our Founding Fathers?

BLUE EYES

My wife and I have breakfast at a local restaurant on Saturday mornings. The specially baked rolls and pastries are a treat, and the variety of coffees is superb. The counter girls are well trained, courteous, and very accommodating. To my surprise, one Saturday morning, the girl waiting on us remarked what beautiful blue eyes I possessed. This is not the first time this has occurred. At a UConn football game, a group of women mistook me for Paul Newman, and gushed over my blue eyes. While walking down Main Street of my hometown, I was complemented by a trio of women over the eye-catching hue of my blue eyes. And, at a Neil Diamond concert at the Hartford Civic Center, sitting next to a group of young women smoking pot and drinking beer, flustered over the blueness of my eyes. I encouraged their platitudes, but my wife would curtail my enthusiasm with a sharp rebuke. There were other occasions that I now recall. The teaching nuns at my parochial school would complement me over my high grades and would slip in an admiring complement over my blue eyes. As a young sailor during World War II, on liberty at San Francisco waiting to catch my ship, passing school girls would giggle and laughingly allude to that blue-eyed handsome sailor. There was an occasion when my eyes became secondary. At a policemen's ball in my hometown, a slightly tipsy woman would come up to me, stroke my hair, touch my nose, and warmly remark how she loved my Roman nose. There were repercussions, as my friends for years would call me "Caesar." My friend, Chuck, and I were discussing old girlfriends over a couple of beers. He asked what I most remembered. I said their smiles. He said, "Nope. The eyes." Let me tell you where it all began. With that little girl in the 5th grade. During recess on the playground, she would skip by and smilingly say, "I love your blue eyes, John."

LIGHT MOMENTS DURING WAR

After boot camp, we were formed into Battery 415, four 40mm anti-aircraft gun crews. We trained at a beach in Virginia, firing at a target sleeve towed by a plane for 30 days. Then caught a train to San Francisco, where we shipped out to New Caledonia. Waiting to catch our ship, we were trucked to the docks to help unload ships. Alongside the road leading to the docks, Japanese prisoners captured on Guadalcanal were held. We would fill our pockets with rocks and stone them as we passed, with accompanying shouts of profanity. Catching another transport, we would board our ship, the U.S.S. Whitney in Purvis Bay in the Solomons. We dumped our garbage outside the sub-net. On a garbage run, a speeding destroyer would cruise by dropping depth charges on a suspected Japanese sub, but almost blowing us up with it. The garbage dumping ground was infested with sharks. Marines on half-tracks would come out and target practice on the sharks or would attach a piece of meat unto a hand grenade, suspended on a thin wire, and blow the shark to pieces when he swallowed it. Ships were not allowed to dump their garbage into the harbor. It was stored in a garbage chute suspended from the fantail. A flat garbage scow would collect it. Ships assigned a few men to man the scow, and became targets by ship's crew that released the garbage from the chutes and would splatter everywhere. I would join the coxswain in the wheelhouse to keep out of harm's way.

When we reached the Philippines, an LST came alongside for repairs, being heavily damaged by enemy fire. When the LST lowered its landing ramp, the captain gave orders for the crew to go recreational swimming. When wise guys of the crew kept yelling "SHARK," scaring the hell out of everybody, the captain rescinded the order. At Tacloban, I was assigned to a whale boat to pick up the mail. While ashore, the coxswain and I commandeered two "Bum" boats, small native fishing sculls, and raced each other offshore. The native owners would reprimand us in their language, but we just shrugged, faking we didn't understand.

We cracked our rudder in a fierce storm, and limped into Sydney, Australia for much needed R & R. Food aboard ship was bland, but we feasted on steak and eggs while ashore. Bars closed at 4 pm due to an alcohol shortage. At closing time, we would load the end of the bar with glasses of beer and would invite Australian soldiers to join us. We had to convert to Australian money. Our last night ashore, we caught a taxi back to the ship, and gave the driver all our loose money, making him the richest driver in town.

When the war ended, our separation center was at Lido Beach, Long Island. We were discharged late in the afternoon, too late to catch a train home, as the last bus left at 6 pm. So a friend and I decided to spend the night in the City. We encamped to the cocktail lounge of the hotel, and sipped champagne cocktails all night to celebrate our end of war and military life. In the morning, we would eat a hearty breakfast and catch a train home. What followed was material for a few very interesting novels.

WAYWARD PRIESTS PREY AS PARISHIONERS PRAY

Servants of Christ are called on to preach His Gospel and walk in His footsteps. Many do, and they are the ones hurt most when their brothers enter the back door. The church of Fairfield County has had its share, abetted by bishops who feign ignorance, or are scared of exposure. It started with Bishop Curtis, who imitated Colonel Clink, "I know nothing." Bishop Egan would develop myopia while his priests held a field day on innocent children. But Bishop Lori, imbued so deep in prayer, he could not hear the shingles being blown off the steeple. He sleepwalked thru the scandals of Father Jude Fay of St. John's, Noroton, and Father Michael Moynihan of St. Michael's of Greenwich. Both would cohabitate with their lovers right in the rectory, plus steal millions of dollars. Throw in the latest case of Father Kevin Wallin (Advocate, 1/23/13), who staged cross-dressing bashes right in the rectory, and you have a trifecta. I must also mention, Bishop Lori spent over a million dollars to keep payments to children sexually abused by his pedophile priests from publication. Such diademical watchfulness, such astute vigilance, gained the bishop a return to the Diocese of Baltimore from whence he came. Former Bishop Bernard Law of Boston was run out of town under similar circumstances only to be promoted in Rome as the curia sang, "How Many Miles to Babylon." Bishop Mahoney of Los Angeles, who built a glass cathedral to himself, would cover up many of his pedophile priests by saying, "I could have been more vigilant." How many treasuries in Baltimore will be emptied for Lori to gain his Red Hat?

Do you know where all this crumbling started? With the onset of Vatican II when many good priests and nuns left the church for the promises of secular life that proved to be illusional. When all reverence disintegrated as the Latin Mass was replaced with the vernacular. It also fostered the idea among bad priests that remained that they could get away with predatory behavior. And they did, because bishops turned a blind eye, or were too scared to correct it. Jesus foresaw the deviancy that would infiltrate his growing church. You will find it in one of His most profound sayings, "When the Son of Man comes, will He find faith left on Earth?"

TAMING BULLIES

I imagine that sometime in their lives, everyone has had an experience with a bully. I would write about my experience with bullies, both as a youngster, and aboard ship during World War II. My son "Casey" would also thrash a bully who picked on his kid sister in high school. I would also witness a bar bully get a thorough whipping one Saturday night. But I would also see the meanest bully of them all receive the beating of his life from one he tormented.

Coming home from the war, my friends and I would have a few beers, and the most delicious grinders, at a local tavern. It was also a place where workers from the local slaughter house would gather for lunch. Among them was Peter A., a bully who would torment and beat anyone he chose. What made him terrifying was his club hand that he injured while working in a grain mill. He also had a dog called "Crackers" that he would send after us that tore our trousers and bit our legs. Carl S. ("Lalo") was one of our group. He was a little older, quiet, unassuming that masked his courage. Pete picked on him before, but he endured the taunts. One day, he drew the line and stood up to Pete, and he challenged him to a fist-fight. Nearby was a grain storage set near a creek. The bar emptied to witness the beating Lalo was to receive. The crowd was shocked to see the results. Lalo would administer the beating that would put an end to Pete's bullying. To put a stamp on the beating, Lalo would smash Pete through the boards of the building where he landed in the mud of the nearby creek. Lalo would be admired and become the talk of the town for years. Lalo's courage would rub off on me, as I had my own encounters with bullies.

YALE AND U-CONN

My oldest brother Walter, we called him "Bud," was an ardent fan of Yale football. We lived in Middletown (25 miles from New Haven), but my brother and a friend would drive to the Yale Bowl and take me along when the Eli Bulldogs played at home. This was during the Great Depression in the 1930's. Yale football was a top team at that time and played teams from all over the country (Michigan, Minnesota, Georgia). It was part of the Ivy League, which contained teams of Columbia, Penn, Cornell, Princeton, and Dartmouth. But the greatest rivalry was with Harvard. Yale Bowl seated 80,000, and you were lucky to get a ticket for that game. Yale also played Army and Navy, and when the Cadet Corp marched into the Bowl at halftime, it was the most spectacular and patriotic inducing feeling you could ever experience. Yale would produce many All-Americans. I would see All-American half-back Clint Frank, and end Larry Kelly, play many times. Columbia would feature All-American quarterback Sid Luckman, while Penn produced Half-back Francis Xavier Reagan and linebacker Ray Nitchske. We were called up to serve during WWII, and when we returned our interest would turn to Wesleyan and U-Conn. My wife and her father were U-Conn alumni and had season tickets to football and basketball.

When our children grew up, three of them would also attend U-Conn. We would meet them at the stadium, watch the game, and then take them out to dinner. Our oldest son, "Casey," was the high school state mile champion and received a full track scholarship to Keene State College in New Hampshire. We would attend his cross-country meets when the fall foliage was at its peak. After the meet, we would take him to dinner and spend the night in a local motel. It was a blessing to watch the children compete in athletics in high school and college. That blessing still continues as we now watch the grandchildren compete in high school and amateur athletics. While growing up, I was not very big or strong. One day, one of my older brothers said to me, "Why don't you start feeding on meat and potatoes, maybe you'll get big enough and strong enough so that I can come to the Yale Bowl to see you play football." Never happened, but the children and grandchildren came close.

GUN CONTROL

Because of the tragedy at Sandy Hook, today's news is beset by
the call to ban all guns. There was a time when gun ownership
was common and a rite of passage. I grew up on the banks of the
Connecticut River in my hometown of Middletown during the Great
Depression. Game was plentiful along the river, and hunting and
fishing were more than a sport as they supplied food for the dinner
table. Favorites were the berry sweetened partridge (Ruffled Grouse).
Coming home from the war, the urgency for hunting diminished.
When I left my hometown and moved to Stamford, I gave my
shotgun and rifle to my brother. However, I still kept my .22 caliber
pistol that I used to shoot rats at the city dump. Coming to the big
city, I felt the need of protection from home break-ins. As our family
grew, my wife demanded I dispose of the gun, fearing the children
might find it and harm themselves. I kept the gun well hidden, but
the constant pleading of my wife overcame my reluctance, and I sold
it to a licensed gun dealership. Home invasions have increased, and I
feel uncomfortable without a gun for family protection. I agree that
gun ownership can be a source of danger. But if the legal ownership
is forced to turn in their weapons, what do we do about the illegal
guns in the hands of criminals?

SOFTBALL GREAT FRANK GROCKOWSKI

I was saddened to hear of the passing of Frank Grockowski on May 18, 2011. Frank and I were close friends and teammates on the Brass Rail Brewer softball team in the late 1940's and early '50's. Led by the pitching of Adam Bula, Ed Mickucki, and "Michigan" Wiernasz, the Brewers were one of the top softball teams in the state, vying for the state championship against the New Britain Emeralds, and their top hurler, Fred Serafini. Serafini and Joe Pisa would be elected to the Connecticut Fastpitch Softball Hall of Fame. The Brewers were managed by the late Myer Fields and Frank "Kelly" Mikucki. Stellar pitching, outstanding defense, and power-hitting carried the Brewers to many state and city championships. Wally Sennik, Joe Pisa, Chet Krajewski, and Ray Wasowicz carried the offense, while "Stash" Krol, Pete Kalinowski, "Smitty" Mikucki, and Frank Grockowski led a tight defense. Hubbard Park was the home field for the Brewers, and the bank of Main Street Extension bordered left field. It was quite a clout to hit a ball to that left field bank, and I saw only two players manage that feat: Wally Sennik and Joe Faggione I consider Joe Faggione the greatest all-around athlete Middletown produced.

Frank Grockowski and Joe Pisa were fiery, full of pepper; constant motion that provided leadership on the field that kept the team at high charge where you could feel the sparks. Charlie Krajewski was the team publicist who would eventually work part-time as a sports reporter for the Middletown Press.

Softball grew in popularity after World War II. Every city had a great team that made competition on a high level statewide that drew great crowds. Frank Grockowski was a highly skilled softball player who helped make the Brass Rail Brewers one of the top teams in the state.

AN OLD FAHIONED SOUTH END OLD TIMERS TRIBUTE

John Cubeta was told he was too small to be selected for a tryout for the Middletown High School football team. It broke his heart. He would come home from the war as a decorated Marine, having fought on Iwo Jima. After the war, most cities would field semi-pro football teams and compete statewide. Johnny would join the Middletown Blue Jackets and lead them to become one of the strongest teams in the state. They played on Sunday afternoons at Municipal Field, and large crowds would attend the games. They really came to watch John—old # 81—perform.

When John had the football, he ran with heart, and boldness, and daring. He not only ran to the end zone—he ran to the river, and he ran to the hills, and he ran to all the landmarks that make our city great. John gave this city one of the greatest football Sundays ever seen at Municipal Field. I won't cite the statistics, because numbers are not important when you enunciate greatness. Just close your eyes and visualize old Number 81 running up and down that field with wind and fire and spirit. He won the day, he won the field, he won the game, he won the city, and he won a place in history. There were days when he ran the opposition right onto their bus. John made destiny runs . . . runs you never forget . . . the kind that make you smile as you grow older. Like Joe Pisa fielded a softball . . . Art Warmsley ran track . . . Ed Mikucki and "Michigan" Wiernasz pitched . . . Wally Sennik hit the long ball . . . and Eddy "Mulligan" Burek ran the basketball court.

There is majesty in sport no matter what level you play. Johnny was an obscure son of the South End when he came upon the football scene. He left no footprints in high school or college. That is why nobody saw him coming. But when he did, he blindsided the world. John now belongs to that special fraternity that graces the wall of the Middletown Sports Hall of Fame. He honors his talent, he honors his sport, he honors his neighborhood, but most of all, he honors the South End Old Timers Athletic Association.

COME ON, GET ANGRY—I AM

Let me awaken your anger, stir your emotions, and arouse you to action for a good cause. The cause is opposition to the arrogance and excesses of the National Endowment for the Arts. First, you must read George F. Will's column on the NEA titled, "Cuts aren't the Cause of Art Degradation." Mr. Will writes, "'The arts,' laments Rep. Sidney Yates (D., IL), 'will be terribly, terribly hurt by the enormous impact of the 5% cut in the NEA's $174.6 million budget.'" What a sycophant. What is really hurtful here is the rending of the moral fabric of our society. Even with the cut, the NEA budget is $39 million larger than federal funding for prevention of breast and cervical cancer. Women of America, where forth is thy indignation? And, good citizens of America, do you know how your tax dollars are being spent by the NEA? Well, let me tell you. Your monies are being used by the NEA to fund art exhibits that confront "taboo issues of gender and sexuality." Do you know what is being displayed? Let me tell you. They feature "abject materials" such as: dead animals, menstrual blood, rotten food, a 3-feet-high mound of synthetic excrement, a film showing a man pushing his head into another man's rectum, and framed samples of an infant's fecal stains. Are you mad enough? Well, hold on, there is more. Highlighting these exhibits are Robert Mapplethorpe's "Self Portrait," a photo of him with a bullwhip in his rectum, and Andres Serrano's "Piss Christ," a photo of a crucifix in a jar of urine. These should get you going, since your hard-earned tax dollars are used to defray expenses. While causes such as crime, drugs, health, education, and poverty go under-funded. When Mr. Serrano was asked to explain the sign-value of his so-called "art," he said, "It's very hard for me as a human being to put a value on these fluids . . . I accept my bodily fluids, and I think Jesus Christ did, too." WOW!!! Sheer impugnity. Blatant irreverence. And I am furious because my tax dollars have given him a platform. Pinch your nose at the nifty verbiage, and recognize Mr. Serrano's words for what they really are. An impingement on reverence. No one has the right to foist their irreverence on others, especially thru the use of public funds. My suggestion to Mr. Serrano is, since he holds his excretions as priceless and acceptable, perhaps he should drink them. After all, recycling is a more recognized use of waste. I burn inside at the audacity of the NEA to deem wholesome, pornography, scatology, and deviate behavior. And I continually am amazed at the urgency of the moral mobilization of this country over issues such as, Save the Whales. While only a few bold individuals and groups will rise to protest the insidious flaunting of the NEA. I believe it is time to bring the NEA on line, to make them conform to code, to pull the reins and shout, "WHOA!!!" Make them conform to the code of decency adhered to by the majority of citizens in this great nation. We are slowly but surely losing some of that greatness, because we good citizens (you and me) have failed to act in the past. If the NEA is allowed to run on, unimpeded, I fear for what lies beyond the rise of tomorrow. The way to achieve desired results on issues that we find intrusive on our sanctity is to make our elected officials in Washington know how we feel. We must get our conversations of displeasure out of the living and dining rooms, taverns, street corners, automobiles, locker rooms, and backyards, and into the offices of our legislators. Tell them we are unhappy with the way the NEA has been allowed to "run the show" with disdain. And we will hold them accountable next election. The answers do not lie with Donahue, Oprah, Geraldo, Sally Jesse, or Ted Koppel. They lie with us. Do not cry tomorrow if you fail to act today. I recall the wisdom of my father, who once told me: Two things happen to you when you lay down, both of them bad. You get stepped on, or you get screwed. What is your choice?

CHANGE IN EDUCATION LED TO BULLYING

The bully-driven suicide of Phoebe Prince has brought to the surface how widespread and unchecked bullying in our schools has become. Citing this tragedy, Nancy Gibbs in the Essay page of TIME magazine, defines when bullying crosses the line from cruel to criminal. She asks why the bullies were not restrained? Too often, parental and administrative failures are dismissed as feigned ignorance or with the excuse that bullying is an insoluble inter-student problem. Just look at the excuses regarding Miss Prince's mother's ignored pleas for help. This is echoed by Edward Boiselle, South Hadley school board chairman, saying, "Some people have unreasonable expectations of what schools can do to stop such tragedies." This is no small deviation from the truth. It is a cowardly equivocation of his elected responsibility—far from a bold footprint for protecting students in his care. When you profess ignorance of your duty of office, you verge on criminal negligence.

There are no behavioral problems injurious to children that cannot be rectified. Yet we are told bullying has no resolution. When tragedy occurs, administrators crawl under that rock, seeking wiggle room to slip blame and deflect charges of dereliction. Where is that leadership that "knows the way, goes the way, shows the way?"

Do you know when our educational system went from steadfast discipline to that mushy concept of self-esteem primacy? When it diverted from the quest of fulfillment by time-honored practices to egg-hunt frivolity? As a WWII veteran attending school under the G.I. Bill, I was an education major when the convergence began in the 1950's. Dictated by "My Pedagogic Creed" by John Dewey, it dismantled the structures of conventional teaching, insisting the past was sinister but the future would be utopian. No more whacks in the back of the head of miscreants. You must softly talk them down from the tree of misbehavior. Being schooled in the trenches, my wild will was not easily breached, forcing me to change majors.

This new order of liberating learning planted the seeds for the rising tide of bullying, which can carry into adulthood. As parents, teachers, authority figures, we must all effect behavior appropriate to a civil and respectful environment. Failure will lead to more Phoebe Prince tragedies, a day when something inside all of us died with her.

Bullies were rare in my high school days (1939-1943). But we knew how to end their reign of terror. Read my letter to the editor, "Handling Bullies," which ran in this newspaper of Feb. 24, 2009. It will make you smile.

The following is Mr. Gawlak's above-referenced letter:

HANDLING BULLIES

The ancient Greeks gave us democracy and knowledge and culture and wisdom and philosophy and war as redeeming qualities. Aristotle said, "You must live life forward, but you can only understand it backward."

Let me take you backward to my time. A time of the Great Depression, and that Great War, of which I helped write a chapter. To my hometown (Middletown), and my high school days (1939-1943), and the bully I engaged.

The insidious infiltration of school bullies has been long and constant. Like an alcoholic, one shove is too many and 100 not enough. They suck the life out of what should be a memorable school experience for many students.

Let me tell you about our remedy. Our bully was named "Smitty," menacing, snarling, hulking. He'd push us smaller kids around, stuff us into lockers, toss our books down the hallways. We were tough neighborhood kids who could handle ourselves with equals. But engaging the bully in a fist fight? Our reason subdued our courage, as the cost would be too great.

One of our crowd was "Jumbo" J.—a tough farm kid and a match for the bully. We didn't hide behind him, but called him when we needed help. We lived by the code, "In the alley after school, there just ain't no golden rule." So one day after school, Jumbo applied this code to Smitty. We were never bullied again. Won't work today. In this insanely litigious society, the bully is favored. You end up on the wrong end of a suit.

There is an epilogue to this story. I left school early to join the Navy. After the war, I reported to Pier No. 92, after a 30-day leave, and then transferred to the Brooklyn Navy Yard to serve my last two months. In the chow line one day, someone grabbed me in a bear hug with the warmest greetings. It was "Smitty," the former bully. The uniform made us equals. On weekends, we rode the train home together. He insisted I had to have supper at his house at least one evening. He said his mother's pasta was the best I'd ever taste. He was right.

We would run into each other after we were discharged. Have a few beers, the best of friends. We still are. Here's to "Smitty" and "Jumbo" and a happy ending to a bully story. How did yours end?

UCONN'S SHAME

The new bark of the UConn Husky has become, "Win baby, win, let the dollars roll in." It is chiseled on the entry gate of our flagship university. And it has become the spirited cheer at Gampel Pavilion and the Hartford Civic Center—the new Novocain that deadens right, and free-floats wrong.

In response to the headlines concerning the latest basketball recruiting scandal involving Nate Miles, listen to the blame-free dodge. First, Coach Jim Calhoun: "It's possible mistakes were made in the recruitment process." Then Athletic Director Jeff Hathaway: "UConn is fully committed to NCAA rules compliance."

This is flapdoodle. These are not sobs coming from the confessional. They both lied and cheated, coming off as two stars aligned in brazen, bald-faced obfuscation. And the NCAA Rules Committee has just slapped them upside the head with the charge: "Failure to promote an atmosphere of compliance."

To remove the dungy odor from themselves, they fire two assistants, reincarnating the role of Pontius Pilate, washing his hands as he sends Jesus to the cross.

Lew Perkins, former UConn athletic director, was one step ahead of the posse when he left for Kansas. Do you believe Hathaway and Calhoun will follow? Baloney! You know why? Because the state Legislature, the UConn governing board, the alumni and the general public wet their pants when faced with confronting this malversation.

As our athletic programs grow, so will our problems. Wasn't a football player stabbed to death on campus last fall?

SOUTH END OLD TIMERS HOLD FINAL REUNION

The South End Old Timers Athletic Association of Middletown held its final reunion on Saturday, Nov. 7, 2009.

The Enders held their first reunion at the Elks Lodge in October 1996.

Chartered in 1995, the original Board of Directors members were: Art Warmsley, Charlie Krajewski, Joe Pisa, John Cubeta, Tony Spada, Ed Siecienski, and Frank Gronckowski, who elected John P. Gawlak as Chairman. Lucy Betterncourt, Fran Patnaude, Ray Wasowicz, Hal Crotty, and Bob Wamester would be added in ensuing years.

The purpose of the organization was to honor individuals, teams, and groups from throughout the city that played during the 1930's, '40's, and '50's. A former sports editor of the Middletown Press, Fred Post, was the organization's historian and publicist.

Membership consisted mainly of individuals who resided in the South End neighborhood, and played on teams in the area. All sports were represented and included the following teams: Scarlet Phantoms, Polish Knights, Otis Cardinals, South End A.C., Walnut A.C. Silver A.C., Duck Hollow Orioles, Hillsides, Brass Rail Brewers, St. Mary's Basketball, and the YMCA Varsity and House Basketball Leagues. Many of these teams were of championship caliber and produced may athletes who have been inducted into the Middletown Sports Hall of Fame.

A special tribute was paid to Charlie Krajewski and Joe Pisa who are widely known and respected in the sports history of Middletown. They were the leading voices in organizing the Old Timers, and involved in city-wide fraternal and athletic organizations.

During the Depression, the YMCA reached out to needy neighborhood youth and encouraged to form a social club and engage in gym and swim activities. After World War II, it became the meeting place for returning veterans who were provided with recreational and athletic opportunities to ease the difficult transition back to civilian life.

In 2001, the YMCA partnered with the South Enders to dedicate the World War II Wall of Honor. The centerpiece was a special plaque honoring eleven members who made the supreme sacrifice during the war. They are: Stanley Dobrinski, Joseph Erlick, Sebastione Faggione, Edmund and Julian Gadzinski, Paul Ribera, William "Shorty" Roguski, Louis Ruffino, Stanley "Socko" Sokolowski, Anthony Sledzick, and Fred Young. Also on display in the YMCA's historic Hazen room is a variety of photos, news clippings, and mementos highlighting the athletic involvement of boys and young men who lived in the South End neighborhood and considered the YMCA a second home.

Many South Enders are graduates of St. Mary's school, and it was a comfort to have Father Marek Masnicki give the invocation and benediction. Frank Sumpter, Executive Director of the YMCA, extolled the long relationship the Old Timers have had with the YMCA. Plans are being formulated to again honor the eleven fallen comrades named on the wall of honor.

SOVIETS, U.S. ARE KEYS TO SUCCESS IN SEOUL

Since the end of World War II, the Olympic Games have been beset with turmoil and uncertainty, due to the political intrigue and military intransigence of the Soviet Union. Until that time, there never has been a boycott, or the constant threat of disruption so prevalent, until the Russians started to flex their newfound international hierarchy. The only other dark time was in the 1936 Summer Games in Berlin, when Hitler raised the spectre of "Aryanism," the ultimate form of racism, that was shattered by the feats of Jesse Owens.

Today, we see the same ominous signs, and the fate of the 1988 Summer Games in Seoul, Korea are precarious. The daily scenes of violence on the streets of Seoul, due to political unrest, cast a shadow upon the future of the Olympics.

The wisdom of selecting Seoul as the site of the 1988 Games, a city of unsettled politics, is without precedent. The unrest and political instability is not new, and has been ongoing since the end of the Korean War. If you have been following the march of history in that country, this should be very clear to you.

I may have been fortunate to attend the last of the peaceful Olympics, as we have known them. My wife, Carol, and I were in Los Angeles during the 1984 Games, the XXIIIrd Olympiad. Our primary purpose for being there was to represent the Stamford YMCA at the 10th World YMCA Health and Physical Education Consultation.

This consultation is held every four years at the site of the Summer Games. Delegates from YMCA's all over the world gather to join in fellowship, share information, and discuss issues of common concern. This meeting helps develop better understanding among national member YMCAs of the World YMCA Alliance, by sharing new and successful health, fitness, nutrition, recreation and sports experiences and developments.

All meetings were held in the mornings to allow the delegates to attend Olympic activities of their choosing. My wife and I attended men's and women's volleyball and gymnastics. The color, the drama, the level of competition, and sincere display of respect and sportsmanship among the athletes, and the elaborate preparation and festivities at the sites of competition were Utopian.

Being in the midst of this pageantry induced an inner patriotism that defies description. You cheered all of our "kids" wearing red, white, and blue as if they were family.

We had the privilege of conversing and becoming friendly with fellow YMCA professionals from Japan, Africa, Venezuela, Brazil, England, Ireland, Germany, and especially Korea. All our conversations ended with a question: would we be seeing each other again in Seoul in 1988?

It was my privilege to become acquainted with Chun Dai Lyun, Executive Director of the Seoul YMCA, who would be hosting the 11th World YMCA Health and Physical Education Consultation. We talked at length about the upcoming Olympic Games, and ramifications of political instability in his country, and the ever-present threat from the covert military regime to the north. Lyun continually assured me that there would be nothing to fear, and the Games would go on in peaceful circumstances.

By nature, all YMCA personnel are idealistic and politically naïve. They see the good in everyone, and in all things. This is the essential attribute that differentiates those who chose the YMCA as a career from the rest. But, the reality of the daily violence and confrontation in the streets of Seoul forebodes uncertainty and misgivings.

Since the 1976 Summer Games in Montreal, the Olympics have been in crisis. The United States boycotted the Summer Games in Moscow because of the Russian invasion of Afghanistan. The Soviet Union and the Eastern Bloc nations boycotted the 1984 Summer Games in Los Angeles just to get even. Now the 1988 Games are in jeopardy for everyone. A change in site may save the Games if a decision is reached early enough to allow for adequate preparations. If a change in site is requested, don't order your tickets just yet, as the Russians may boycott if the site is unacceptable to them. The Soviet Union has already alluded to the possibility of withdrawing from the Games at Seoul. Don't be surprised if they are found to be behind some of the violence, as they thrive on turmoil and revel in disruption. The Russians would love to see Western ideology embarrassed, no matter where it exists.

The 1984 Summer Games in Los Angeles renewed a diminishing pride and lethargic patriotism in this country. Under the leadership of Peter Ueberroth, the Games were thrilling, well managed, and the most financially successful of any Olympiad, winter or summer.

But, do you realize that we have not faced the Russians in Olympic competition since 1976? It will be 12 years in 1988. And, if things go wrong, which is what is happening, it will be 16 years (1992) for another opportunity, and maybe never. Our athletes compiled the highest number of Olympic medals ever at Los Angeles. But, the competition from the Soviet Union, East Germany, Cuba and others were missing. If you are to be the best, you must compete against the best. The Russians and the Eastern Bloc nations produce some of the best athletes in the world in gymnastics, swimming, track and field, volleyball, weightlifting, boxing, water polo—and, don't forget, they even beat us in men's basketball in Munich.

There is still hope that the Games of the XXIVth Olympiad will be held in Seoul. For that to happen, it is my studied judgment that the following steps need to be taken:

1. The United States must exert its influence on the South Korean leaders to allow for a more open society with guaranteed individual freedom, and political safeguards for free and open elections. The threat of economic sanctions and a trade embargo will accomplish this.

2. The Soviet Union must assert pressure on the volatile and hostile military regime of North Korea to diminish its pugnacity and collusion. I feel a greater threat for disruption of the Games can come from the north. A backhand slap can accomplish this.

3. The United States and the Soviet Union must cooperate in lending leadership to overcome the ongoing problems in Seoul. They must be the intercessors and not the abettors.

These things must happen if there is to be a safe and sodalitous Olympics in Seoul. If the two biggest guys in town cannot or will not stop a street fight, then we are in trouble.

I question the feasibility of moving the Games to an alternate site, even at this early date. The logistics are too overwhelming, when you consider that four years are usually needed for site preparation. The safest place to hold the Games would be Moscow. Who would dare taunt the neighborhood bully, especially in his own backyard?

If the Games are canceled in Seoul, it portends the end of the Olympic movement as we know it. I would then agree with Howard Cosell that the Games be moved to a permanent and neutral site. My vote would be for Greece, where the Olympics originated, and where King Zeus still reigns, and even the gods fear his displeasure.

BARACK'S BAD BUDS

If people are best judged by the company they keep, then Barack Obama has got some explaining to do. There's his long-term relationships with extremist preachers like Jeremiah Wright and Michael Pfleger. And his association with '60's radical terrorists William Ayers and Bernardine Dohrn.

And then there's his links with Tony Rezko—the Chicago political power broker who faces up to 20 years in prison after his conviction last week on 16 counts of wire fraud, mail fraud, money-laundering and soliciting bribes.

Rezko was found guilty of corrupting two state boards as part of a scheme in which he collected millions in kickbacks from companies seeking government contracts. Rezko, prosecutors charged, was "the man behind the curtain, pulling the strings."

The Obama-Rezko ties aren't ideological—they're just old-fashioned Chicago street politics at work.

Over the years, Rezko has raised as much as a quarter of a million dollars for Obama's political campaigns.

The now-presumptive Democratic nominee also did some legal work for Rezko early on, helping him earn millions developing run-down housing properties, many of them located in Obama's state Senate district. (More than *half* of those properties have since fallen into foreclosure, incidentally.)

But there's a far more personal connection, as well.

In 2005, Rezko helped Barack and Michelle Obama by buying a lot they could not afford next to the new home they'd just bought, then selling them part of the property so they could build a fence.

Obama admits that, at the time, he already knew that Rezko "was going to have some significant legal problems" with his housing deals. He now calls their personal transaction "a boneheaded move."

Indeed it was.

All in all, Obama apparently was one of the few people in Chicago who was blind to the fact that Tony Rezko was a key political-influence peddler.

Just as he was about the only person in Trinity United Church who missed every one of Jeremiah Wright's regular militant anti-American sermons.

No wonder Obama's reaction to Wednesday's jury verdict was, "This isn't the Tony Rezko I knew"—just as he maintained that Wright's now-infamous diatribe was "not the person I met 20 years ago."

All of which makes us wonder: What *did* Barack Obama really know?

And when did he really know it?

A CATHOLIC CRISIS, BESTOWED FROM ABOVE

The nation's Roman Catholic priests will not miss the year 2002, their annus horribilis. A year ago, few could have imagined the disrepute into which the priesthood would slip following hundreds of sexual abuse cases involving clergy and a clueless response by bishops who misidentified exactly whom there were supposed to be shepherding.

The anger was intense enough to destroy not just a few ecclesiastical careers but also the goodwill of parishioners and the public that priests used to take for granted. Almost forgotten are my former colleagues, the hard-working core of priests who are not malefactors. These men remain trapped in a system where they have next to nothing to say about the shape of Catholic leadership or its response to the crisis.

Little wonder that priests' numbers are dwindling. Their experience, their personal holiness and their spiritual insight often don't seem to count. The hierarchy seeks only their silence and deference. As priests see one bishop after another imposed from above to put in place policies without input from the clergy or the laity, they become resigned, disgusted, and just plain tired.

At the same time, a smaller group of clergy ambitious for higher office have long brought all their skills to the challenging task of pleasing their omnipotent superiors rather than responding to the promptings of their subordinates, or of the laity.

In the more than two decades I spent as a priest (I left the clergy a decade ago over the issue of celibacy), I had many opportunities to observe the ways priests are required to grovel to their superiors. Once, back in the seminary, as a hundred or so of us stood around waiting for His Eminence the cardinal to appear for an event, a student approached one of the monsignors. "So, it seems the cardinal is late?" he asked.

"Excuse me, young man," he was told, "the cardinal is never late. Everyone else is early."

Some years later, when I was head of the seminary's student body, I found myself seated next to the archbishop at a dinner. Our student council had recently completed a study of issues affecting seminary life and our future as priests and human beings. I was eager to share its results with the authorities, and here I was, sitting at dinner next to Himself!

But as soon as I broached the topic, the cardinal silenced me. I was not to approach him directly, he said, but only through the appropriate channels so that the chain of authority would be unbroken. He had no desire to know firsthand what his future priests were thinking.

Bishops anointed "by the favor of the Apostolic See," as the Vatican terms it, are deferred to not because of their competence or learning, but because of that favor. This is true today, 40 years after the Second Vatican Council sought to encourage a more collegial style of leadership—one seeking input from clergy and parishioners, and even acknowledging the laity as part of the priesthood.

Accustomed to this deferential thinking, today's mis-managers of the clerical abuse scandal do not see themselves as ill-intentioned. Ignoring the victims of abuse grows out of an ideology that holds that clergy are different from ordinary people. Accountability is for lesser mortals.

The culture of deference to the clerical mystique is deep-rooted. A dozen years ago, I was at a conference for priests on preaching and worship in the context of Vatican II, and the curriculum was suspended one afternoon to make room for an impromptu address by the archbishop. By the end of his hour-long monologue, he had effectively dismissed the newer approaches the faculty had been promoting. Waxing eloquent on the unique power of priests to accomplish things that not even kings and queens could do, he reminded us that even God obeys the words of a priest when he consecrates the bread and wine at mass. There was no rebuttal from the assemble priests.

The trouble with deference and silence, of course, is that they encourage ignorance and denial about issues that need to be addressed.

A few months ago, a group of New York clergy were told by a high-ranking official that he was open to discussing issues directly. However, some of those present told me, it was stressed that this was to be a so-called Roman dialogue, which means: I'll do the talking, you listen.

The seeds of the present crisis were really sown in 1968, the year of the papal encyclical known as Humane Vitae, which began the undoing of Vatican II. The encyclical reasserted the church's opposition to artificial contraception and to the principle that church teaching grows and develops. Catholics were not to decide for themselves, as a matter of conscience, whether to use contraception.

After the encyclical, thousands of priests remained silent about this teaching on birth control—one that was out of sync with the life the faithful lived. Many decided (as the laity had begun to do) that the church's teaching was no real guide for their own sexual lives. Many resigned and sought happiness elsewhere. Others stayed but made their own decisions about licit and illicit sexual relationships—and were silent about it.

Is it possible that this silence—combined with a culture that already valued suppression—fostered the idea among some bad priests that they would get away with predatory behavior?

Over the last year, however, the silence has been shattered by public outcry and the flock's rediscovery of its voice. What remains to be seen is whether these voices will be joined by others from within the clergy—and if they will be allowed to influence the course of Catholic teaching and policy.

From an article by Paul E. Dinter; New York Times, Jan., 2003.

A HOUSE DIVIDED: TWO AMERICAS

Over the past three decades, we have become two Americas. We are no longer one large American family with shared prosperity and shared political and economic power, as we were in the decades following WWII. Today, no common enemy unites us as a nation. No common enterprise, like settling the West or rocketing to the moon, inspires us as a people.

We are today a sharply divided country—divided by power, money, and ideology. Our politics have become rancorous and polarized, our political leaders unable to resolve the most basic problems. Constant conflict has replaced a sense of common purpose and the pursuit of the common welfare. Not just in Washington, but across the nation, the fault lines that divide us run deep, and they are profoundly self-destructive, unless we can find our way to some new unity and consensus. Abraham Lincoln gave us fair warning. "A house divided against itself," Lincoln said, "cannot stand."

From Who Stole the American Dream, by Hedrick Smith.

THE CORRUPTIVE INFLUENCE OF MONEY

Today, the gravest challenge and the most corrosive fault line in our society is the gross inequality of income and wealth in America. Not only political liberals, but conservative thinkers, as well, emphasize the danger to American democracy of this great divide. "America is coming apart at the seams—not seams of race or ethnicity, but of class," writes conservative sociologist Charles Murray, of the American Enterprise Institute.

Murray voices alarm at what he describes as, "The formation of classes that are different in kind and in their degree of separation from anything that the nation has ever known . . . . The divergence into these separate classes, if it continues, will end what has made America, America." In our new economy, America's super-rich have accumulated trillions in new wealth, far beyond anything in other nations, while the middle-class has stagnated. Wealth begets wealth, especially when reinforced through the influence of money in politics.

The danger is that if the extremes become too great, the wealth dichotomy tears the social fabric of the country, undermines our ideal of equal opportunity, and puts the whole economy at risk—and more than the economy, our nation itself.

From Who Stole the American Dream by Hendrick Smith

CONSCIENCE OF COMMUNITY

For 40 years, I have shared a friendship with and had an admiration for John Gawlak, the centerpiece of a recent article by Angela Carella. I have chosen to call him "The Hammer," and he refers to himself as such when he calls me. The appellation is a reference to an ancient proverb which states that "He is a man with a big hammer and treats all problems as if they were nails."

In addition to his writing prowess, John was the heart and soul of the Stamford YMCA, helping to formulate a program of fitness which fulfilled the needs of the diverse population who frequented the YMCA. He was and is a man for all seasons.

It was therefore with an extreme sense of gratitude that I read the article devoted to him, an article which captured his voice speaking out against all forms of injustice. John epitomizes the conscience of the community, and his clarion call, like Thomas Paine, reminds us that "These are the times that try men's souls." He is no summer soldier or sunshine patriot who shrinks from the service of his country.

Author: Franklin Melzer, Stamford Advocate, June 2010.

THE COMPANY THAT BARACK OBAMA HAS KEPT

Forty years ago this month, Paris exploded in left-wing student riots that led to a nationwide general strike. The revolutionary fervor of France's soixante-huitards ('68ers) spread widely, including to American campuses. If you're wondering when the Good '60s of peace, love, and civil rights gave way to the Bad '60s of anarchy and violence, May 1968 is as good a historical pivot point as any.

John McCain was in the Hanoi Hilton at the time. Barack Obama was 6 years old. Yet the restless spirit of '68 haunts this year's presidential campaign, especially the White House bid of Obama, who, having pretty much missed the '60s—"Civil rights, sexual revolution, Vietnam War. Those all sort of passed me by," he told The Atlantic's Andrew Sullivan last year—was supposed to take us beyond those divisive traumas.

It's not working out that way. His former pastor the Rev. Jeremiah Wright is an unreconstructed '60s radical, a fire-breathing disciple of James Cone's period-piece black liberation theology. Obama wrote in his 1995 autobiography, "Dreams From My Father," about his attraction the leftist pastor's church as a vehicle for social change. If black nationalism would uplift the race," he wrote, "then the hurt it might cause well-meaning whites, or the inner turmoil it caused people like me, would be of little consequence."

That's a remarkable admission of a racialized "ends justify the means" morality. It helps explain why Obama was willing to stick with a crackpot like Wright. It also might explain why an up-and-coming Barack Obama found nothing particularly wrong with rubbing political elbows with Bill Ayers, the Chicago university professor and onetime fugitive member of the revolutionary, communist Weather Underground.

Ayers, an unrepentant '60s domestic terrorist, is an academician in good standing and active member of Chicago's progressive community. It is unremarkable that a rising star in Chicago Democratic politics would collaborate with Ayers, which tells us something about the soixante-huitard generation.

They may have failed at revolution, but they succeeded in changing the culture. (A famous soixante-huitard slogan: "Live without limits, and enjoy without restraint.") They did so in large part by, to use the Marxist Antonio Gransci's phrase, "Marching through the institutions." Pulpits. Professorships. Publishing and media. And in some cases, politics.

It's not "guilt by association" to inquire to what extent Obama—whose moral and political conscience was shaped by his education at elite universities, his street activism and his tutelage at Wright's knee—shares the views and assumptions of the soixante-huitards. In terms of style, he's plainly not one of them. But his deeply liberal voting record marks him as at least a fellow traveler. Besides, as Rolling Stone magazine put it last year in a sympathetic profile, Obama's is "as openly radical a background as any significant American political figure has ever emerged from."

This may be of no matter to the left, but Obama is not running for mayor of Berkeley, president of Harvard, or prime minister of The New York Times.

But if the '60s radicals went too far, they had ample cause to protest—especially against the war in Vietnam, which the U.S. government had been lying about and would continue to lie about. The radicals weren't all wrong about American power. Know why the terrorist team of Ayers & Dohrn never went to jail? The FBI broke so many laws trying to catch them that putting them on trial would have been futile.

"By any means necessary" was not just an ethic of the far left (ask Ollie North). Nor is it a thing of the past, as the Bush administration and its allies have so amply demonstrated in relentless pursuit of the president's prerogatives. If it's fair to judge Obama by the ideological company he keeps, then McCain deserves the same. Meaning well is not exculpatory.

That said, Obama's radical baggage is more politically damaging because it deflates the hope many voters invested in him. He was once the man to deliver American politics from the storm and stress of the '60s generation—"Goodbye to all that," as The Atlantic headlined Sullivan's much-read pre-primary encomium to Obama's transformational potential.

Not yet, alas. Against his own conscience, the ambitious but insecure young Obama compromised with the malevolent spirit of '68 for the sake of worldly gain. But the consequences are not proving to be as little as he expected.

Said the Devil to Faust: "In the end, you are exactly—what you are."

Yes.

From an article by Rod Dreher, May, 2008.

SHOOTING CHILDREN IS NOT A SUBJECT FOR DISCUSSION

Since the terrible, unspeakable tragedy at Newtown, the state has been in a constant meeting and publicity frenzy for the elimination of guns, especially high-powered, high-numbered magazines. It was political posturing as Sen. Dick Blumenthal, Gov. Dan Malloy, even President Obama rushed to the scene shouting "we must get rid of the guns!" But right under their noses, it is reported that gun sales by the Sturm Ruger gun maker of Fairfield has jumped by 50% in 2012. The real cause of the sickening slaughter of children was not even mentioned. A mentally ill young man whose treatment was neglected by his parents and school authorities since early childhood escaped the scrutiny that should have been headlined. The mother's insane addiction to high-powered rifles, and her teaching her mentally ill son to use them, gets little mention. The state police report detailing cause and effect is forthcoming. Just what will be the reckoning of the greatest slaughter of our country's school children? Will it skim over the untreated and neglected mental illness of Adam Lanza? The carnage was so sickening, so gruesome, it was indicated in a local newspaper, at the wake of one of the 6-year-old victims, his face was shrouded from his eyes down because his jaw was blown away. It started at Columbine. Where does it end? When does it hit Stamford? I have two grandchildren in schools here, and three more in nearby towns. If the schools can't handle bullying, how can they stop gunfire?

THE SAGA OF A MAVERICK PRIEST

In the history of the modern church, there has never been a more maligned priest then Father Andrew M. Greeley who passed away Wednesday May 29. he was condemned as a reactionary liberal, but he was a sound visionary, and warned about church failings. He was the first to sound the alarm about priestly pedophilia in is home diocese of Chicago, which started the exposure and clean-up all across the country. He wasn't maligned for breaking his priestly vows, stealing church treasures, or preaching a new gospel, but for his liberal views, and many novels containing sexual exploits of his protagonists (priests, family, friends). He would be harshly criticized for calling for the elimination of priestly celibacy, the election of the Pope by the laity, and the poor quality of Sunday homilies.

He would create a writing center that offered eulogies to priests that needed help in the Sunday pulpit. He would receive heat from Rome, calling the Curia the "Lavender Mafia." He preached celibacy should be lifted because Jesus did not mandate it. It was instituted by the ealy church because married priests absconded with church treasuries and property. His relationship with nuns was cool because of his being rapped on his knuckles with a ruler for not holding his pencil right.

Relatively unknown, Father Greeley burst upon the scene when he published his first racy novel. "The Cardinal Sins," a story of two Chcago friends who entered the priesthood. One would become a Cardinal, who engaged in sexual encounters, while his priest friend would criticize him for breaking his vows. He was ostrasized by his diocese for continuing to publish sexy novels, so he fled to the University of Arizona to teach sociology, and do research on various church issues.. His novels were so lucrative he would offer his diocese one million dollars to aid needy parishes. When turned down, he would establish a charity to distribute the funds himself.

Father john Shea, a friend and mentor, would suggest Greeley write a new catechism: instead of applying religious truths of life, search in life for hints that point at religious truths. He would publish: "The Great Mysteries—An Essential Catechism," which was roundly criticized by the hierarchy. He would also publish a more profound, reverent, and spiritually enhancing "Myths of Religion" (the Jesus myth—the Sinai myth—the Mary myth), which was more readily accepted.

While his novels carried sexual misconduct, he remained celibate and true to his calling. He stressed forgiveness though repentance, and the endings of hs novels carried that message. He also inserted profound spiritual instructions that simplified the teachings of Chist: mainly how we are to live to prudently gain access to His Father's kingdom.

CASEY'S REVENGE

Oh, somewhere in this favored land
Dark clouds may hide the sun
And somewhere bands no longer play
And children have no fun

And somewhere over blighted lives
There hangs a heavy pall
But Mudville hearts are happy now
For Casey hit the ball.

From the poem by Grantland Rice, 1907

CHASING THE BLUE'S

Tiny Bubbles,
In the wine,
Make me happy.
Make me feel fine.

Don Ho, Hawaiian Master Minstrel

A WEDDING TOAST TO CHARLIE & KIM

This is a special occasion, and special occasions call for a special story. Indian Lore tells us of the majesty of the eagle; as he soars thru endless space, he carries all of our burdens with him. And when he alights, he disposes our burdens, which carries the promise of good fortune.

One morning, a young brave leaves his tent and sees an eagle soaring by. So he begins to follow him, seeking his good fortune when he sees him land. But, he never comes back. In the after-life, his wife approaches him and asks why he never came home. He tells her, "The eagle never stopped flying."

Now, the ancient Greeks were proponents of wisdom. They wrote, "The splendor of wisdom never sleeps." But wisdom fell asleep for that unfortunate young Indian.

My wish, no, the wish of all of us here, for Charlie and Kim, is that they never let their wisdom fall asleep. That they know when to stop at that juncture, where lore and reason become incompatible.

Let us drink a toast to Charlie and Kim, that they may have a long, lasting, loving, life, and that they inherit the good fortune, as promised by that soaring eagle.

VOICE OF THE PEOPLE—YOU SAID IT:

The Following quotes were printed in the local Stamford Advocate newspaper under the section "You Said It."

MUSIC TO THE EARS

Higher education has been noted for dancing vocabulary. But UConn President Susan Herbst's rant on architectural plans (news story, Aug. 16) to enhance "precious pedagogical ideals" is melodious academia verbiage.

John P. Gawlak

STICK TO SPORTS, LUPICA

Stamford, Conn.: I enjoy reading Filip Bondy and Mike Lupica on the sports page of the Daily News. Bondy is sound, solid, and sensible, and Lupica is king of the sports page. But when he ventures outside of sports, he becomes insulting and engages in doomsday pyrotechnics. Rein it in, Mike. You star on the sports page. Keep it there.

John P. Gawlak

RULES OF THE GAME

Now that the Super Bowl is over, let's talk a little football. Charlie Conerly, former N.Y. Giants quarterback, once said, "When you win, you're an old pro. When you lose, you're an old man.

John P. Gawlak

DOOMED FAMILY

Tragedy is associated with the Kennedy family as happiness is with Brigadoon. The latest? The haunting suicide of Robert F. Kennedy Jr.'s wife, Mary, and the ensuing family feud over her burial.

It seems bad Kennedy episodes are intrinsic. Nothing tops them more than Ted Kennedy's swim at Chappaquiddick. Why do we keep building monuments to people with bad resumes?

John P. Gawlak

BEST SPORTSWRITERS

I've read some great columns by Daily News sportswriters over the years: Dick Young, Jimmy Cannon, Bill Gallo, etc. But you have to put Vic Ziegel's "Memories of My Office That Ruth Built" on Sept. 19 right up there with the best.

John P. Gawlak

TRUE FOR US ALL

Now that football is finished, let's talk basketball. Charles Barkley telling Bob Costas in a TV interview: "The older I get, the faster I was."

John P. Gawlak

THAT'S PRETTY LOW

The New York Daily News reports a huge number of burglaries of homes in the New York area hard hit by Hurricane Sandy. I would label these thieves as lower than whale dung. And that's on the bottom of the ocean.

John P. Gawlak

SANTA IN BLUE

Larry DePrimo, a New York City policeman, digs into his own pocket to buy a shoeless, homeless man a pair of boots with thermal socks (N.Y. Daily News, Nov. 30). "Just out to help," says the officer. Yes, Virginia, there is a Santa Claus.

John P. Gawlak

MADE HER DAY

When the Republican convention erupted into the chant, "Make my Day" as Clint "Dirty Harry" Eastwood skewered President Obama, Peggy Noonan wrote that she would stand it as one of the great convention moments ever.

John P. Gawlak

BOGIE AND OBAMA
Regarding Obama and same-sex marriage: In the movie, "African Queen," when Humphrey Bogart makes a move on Katharine Hepburn, she rebukes him, stating, "You must aspire to higher things." I think President Obama missed the message.

John P. Gawlak

ORATOR IN CHIEF
Why is it with Barack Obama that having a golden voice is the best credential to be elected president? Yet, I once read that linguists are devoid of great ideas.

John P. Gawlak

DON'T FOOL YOURSELF
It is rare for me to dislike someone, but I do not suffer fools. Those who do become one.

John P. Gawlak

PUCKERPUSSES ON PARADE
Stamford, Conn: Hillary Clinton playing kissy-face with Barack Obama is the biggest scam since Judas kissed Christ.

John P. Gawlak

BATTLE FATIGUE
Nothing brought our nation together more soundly and resolutely since World War II than 9/11.
World War II was fought with strength, courage, and determination. The desert wars are so overdrawn in time and resources that the results, like with Korea and Vietnam, will be fruitless.

John P. Gawlak

SPREADING THE WEALTH
Stamford, Conn: You delude yourself if you think the President and Congress run our country. Both are pawns of the super-wealthy. Lobbyists outnumber Congress 130-1. They spend $28.6 billion to buy favors, a 60-1 business advantage. Who do you think scuttles legislation against assault rifles.

John P. Gawlak

GOD'S PUNISHMENT
Killing children is so reprehensible that in Matthew 18, God mandates the punishment for someone who does it: tie a stone around his neck and drown him in the open sea.

John P. Gawlak

JOB ONE
A quote from Jacqueline Kennedy: "If you bungle raising your children, I don't think whatever else you do well matters very much."

John P. Gawlak

INSTITUTION OF MARRIAGE
The Supreme Court is now debating same sex unions. But at Earth's creation, God fashionde Adam and Eve, creating the institution of marriage between a man and woman, commanding them to increase and multiply, fill the Earth and subdue it. Without usurping God's greater wisdom, who can tell me how this command can be fulfilled by joining two Adams . . . or two Eves?

John P. Gawlak

KNOW WHEN TO GO
Yogi Berra, as a guest on Mike Lupica's radio talk show, "Many athletes have never learned that when they are becoming a museum piece rather than a center piece, walking away is a better outcome."

John P. Gawlak

DON'T COMPLAIN
The next time you feel like complaining, remember, your garbage disposal eats better than 90 percent of the world.

John P. Gawlak

SPEECHIFYING
Just how will history record the president's Inaugural address? As more the rhyme of the poet, rather than the rhythm of a nation?

John P. Gawlak

ACTS OF WONDER

I have always marveled at a robin struggling to pull a worm out of the ground. It was equally amazing seeing a robin searching for a worm after a recent snow-fall.

John P. Gawlak

THE ONLY WAY

From the president on down, there has been a lot of grandstanding on gun control. Much of it will be ineffective. The only real solution is to ensure that young people who need mental health treatment receive it at an early age.

John P. Gawlak

CLASS ACT

One of sports' classiest moments was Lou Gehrig's retirement speech at Yankee Stadium. Coach Geno Auriemma's taking the blame for UCONN's loss to Notre Dame Sunday, lifting the burden off his players' shoulders for bungling their late-seconds opportunity to win the game, ranks right up there with the best.

John P. Gawlak

A JOURNAL

OF

FIVE

BROTHERS

AT

WAR

While this is a human interest story of five brothers at war, it really is the story of all veterans of World War II. It has been more than fifty years, but the grunts can still feel the ground shake . . . and the swabs scurry to battle stations at the sound of General Quarters. You see, there is no exit from a war experience . . . it never leaves you. Time never eradicates memories of that cauldron of fire, and smoke, and steel.

Most veterans are reluctant to articulate the story they carry inside. It is too painful. Allow me to write their story. And if I seem too presumptuous, I beg your indulgence. Honors and distinctions belong to all the fine young men and women who were caught up in that web of history . . . who are marked with a special sign . . . who belong to that special fraternity that has heard the cannons in the distance. To those who came back, and those that lie beneath white crosses in distant places. If you have never seen those hallowed grounds, they stretch beyond the horizon, and drain your soul.

My story begins on a chilly April evening in 1943. I was 17, about to graduate from high school. It was around the kitchen table that I told my father I was enlisting in the Navy. All family activities took place around the kitchen table in those days. My father was dismayed and berated me. He reminded me that four brothers were already at war, and that I was needed at home. He was furious that I was leaving school before graduation. He was not as eloquent, but he paraphrased Manuelito, legendary Navajo Chief, "My child, education is the ladder." It is difficult to reason with the young sometimes. But you have to understand the mood of the country after the treachery of Pearl Harbor. Patriotism clutched at your throat, and if you did not rush down to the nearest recruiting station, you might lose your chance at the glory of valor.

I forged my father's name to my enlistment papers, and I was off to join the brothers. Eight weeks of boot camp . . . seven days leave . . . six weeks of anti-aircraft gunnery training . . . then a ship out of San Francisco that did not return until the war was over. While on leave from boot camp, I visited my mother at a tuberculosis sanatorium. She recoiled in fear as she saw her baby in uniform. The brothers and I never saw her again. She died a year later. None of us were able to get home for the funeral. The brothers and I were in areas of combat, and the logistics of getting relieved was unrealistic. For the brothers and all the fine young men of my generation it was Kamikazes and typhoons off Okinawa; Kaitens (Kamikaze submarines) at Ulithi, and See Adler harbor; the bloody beaches and stifling jungles of the Solomons, New Guinea, and the Philippines; the heat and dust of North Africa; and the mud of Italy.

It was a long, hard time coming, but it ended one day. Through the extended ordeal, there was no failure of courage . . . that human equation united us in spirit by a sense of common danger. The brothers and I came home. It was four years for them . . . only three for me. None of us came back whole. We all left a piece of ourselves over there. There was no bitterness . . . only relief. We were proud sons of our Polish heritage; proud sons of our faith; proud sons of this nation; proud and eager to answer the call to duty. What we did was noble in purpose and pure in intent . . . to smite the enemy. When I say this, I recall the words of Homer, "The single best augury is to fight for your country in a noble cause."

Have no illusions about war. It is not a John Wayne movie. War is about killing. Getting the job done, coming home—put your gun away, and enjoy the peace. The ending of hostilities was the source and summit of our belief that the peace won on the battlefield would extend to eternity. But a lot went wrong with the country we loved and the peace we forged from that conflagration.

The brothers and I puzzled over subsequent wars (Korea, Vietnam) . . . stalemate and withdrawal seemed to be the objective. And at home we agonized over the moral failures: the rise of irreverence; the fall of the family' the jading of sexual sanctity; the mias ma of public profanity; the misbegotten obscenities of the entertainment industry. It seemed to be a casual strumming toward the seventh ring of Dante's Inferno. Rioting, looting, the burning of our cities. And the politicos paraded amid the debris and exclaimed, "We do not condone this, but we understand it." Say What??? Abraham Lincoln didn't understand it. Listen to what he said, "There is no grievance that is fit object of redress by mob law."

All the brothers are gone now. They lie under white markers in veterans cemeteries. At their funerals, the bugle sounded, volleys were fired, and the flag folded into that special design that only a fallen warrior would recognize. The brothers did not die of the wounds of war. What killed them was having to observe the stripping of the bark of the moral fiber of our nation. To watch, as the land they loved, slipped the surly bonds of depravity and touched the face of evil. I sometimes hear the brothers calling me, "Get out of there, it's becoming too dangerous."

It was a difficult period of adjustment for all the fine young men who returned. We never had a youth. We went from 17 to 35 overnight. We had no protracted age of innocence. For us, there was no springtime of a young life. Charles Dickens must have had us in mind when he wrote, "For steel to be true, it must pass thru the fire." And for all the fine young men who lie beneath the crosses, I believe they weep for the legacy that was squandered. Shirley Poncini in an op-ed article challenged us when she said, "Be not afraid to root out the evils destroying the soul of man." Greek mythology tells us that fallen warriors of all wars, friend and foe, gather beneath the volcano . . . where they drink from a pit of goats' blood and sharpen their weapons . . . preparing for Armageddon. Then they will rise as a giant armada to engage the forces of darkness.

In the meantime, I see the stirring, of boldness amongst the people of good will. A chorus of calls to reclaim our essential moral foundations. To undo the betrayal of the culture changers. Culture changers who lack moral compass and distort our moral vision. Culture changers who have stolen our peace. And now the sanctimonious cynics, with their golden pens and erudite theses become apologists for our dropping of the atomic bomb . . . theses that impinge on the moral judgment of former president Harry Truman. And I say, dare not subtract from the message of that day, unless you were part of that history. Let no one disparage that decision unless they were part of the gathering forces preparing to invade the Japanese mainland. That invasion would have made Iwo Jima, Okinawa, and D-Day look like a minor skirmish. Sixty-five years ago, the brothers and all the fine young men and women of my generation exemplified the soul of this nation . . . a nation never more united in a single purpose. We still do, though we go quietly into the night.

John P. Gawlak is a resident of Stamford, CT, having served in the U.S. Navy aboard the U.S.S. Whitney, 1943-46, in the South Pacific and the Philippines.

YMCA MEN / FIVE BROTHERS AT WAR

I was the youngest of five brothers who served in World War Two. In April of 1943, at age 17, I walked out of my high school and joined the Navy. My brothers were already overseas, and I felt I had to be there, too.

Soon after boot camp, I boarded the USS Whitney at Noumea, New Caledonia. This was the staging area for the beginning of the island-hopping campaign that started at Guadalcanal and led to the mainland of Japan.

The Whitney was a destroyer tender, attached to a small task force of 4 cruisers and 12 destroyers and all that we had after being decimated at Pearl Harbor. Task Forces 38 and 58 were just being built stateside at the time. We were always close by when the task force went up the line. The action centered on the lower Solomon chain and when the ships returned, we would repair torpedo, bomb, and shell damage, and re-supply them with ammunition and fuel. Some destroyers came back with their bows or fantails completely blown away. Cruisers had gaping torpedo holes mid-ship. Our repairs would allow them to navigate to Pearl Harbor or Sydney, Australia for major reconstruction.

As the campaign moved north and the fleet swelled with newer and bigger ships, we were assigned to the 7th fleet under Admiral William "Bull" Halsey. The Admiral would later cite our ship with a letter of commendation. We cracked our rudder in a fierce storm and limped into Sydney to be re-fitted and for much-needed R & R.

Our itinerary took us from New Caledonia to the Hebrides, the Solomons, New Guinea, the Admiralty Islands, and finally to the Philippines. When the war ended, I chose to come home rather than stay with the ship to join the occupation forces in Tokyo Bay.

While we were at Manus (November, 1944), a Japanese suicide submarine, a Kaiten, snuck into the harbor and blew up the USS Mount Hood, an ammunition ship. We were moored one mile away, and the shock wave was tremendous, the devastation to ships within a half-mile was indescribable. I was to learn later that five friends of mine from my hometown were lost with the "Hood." All my brothers returned home safely, some wounded, all decorated. For me, it was three hard years at sea, and I found it took only one day at war to be robbed of my innocence.

USS Mount Hood Explodes

Joseph W. Gawlak

Stanley A. Gawlak

John P. Gawlak

Joseph W. Gawlak

Peter P. Gawlak

Paul L. Gawlak.

Paul L. Gawlak

WAR CHRONOLOGY

1. Joe—would fight his way across North Africa, and up the Italian peninsula with the Eighth Armored Division where he would capture a Nazi flag.
2. Peter—would carry supplies with the Merchant Marine thru Nazi submarine packs in the Murmansk Run, and dodge Nazi bombers in the Mediterranean.
3. Paul—with the First Cavalry Division would fight in New Guinea and capture a Japanese flag in the Philippines.
4. Stan—aboard the light cruiser USS Milwaukee would be part of the task force to chase the German battleship Graf Spee into Montevideo where it was scuttled. He would come out to the South Pacific aboard the heavy cruiser USS Vincennes and survive a typhoon and dodge kamikazes off Okinawa.
5. John—would witness a Japanese suicide submarine (a Kaiten) blow up the ammunitions ship USS Mount Hood in the Admiralty Islands. His ship would receive a letter of commendation from Admiral William "Bull" Halsey, Commander of the Seventh Fleet.

Exploring the "Deep" is fascinating, revealing, and dangerous.

PRIDE OF THE SOUTH END

Here are three life-long friends who grew up in the same neighborhood during the Great Depression, went to school together, played ball together, went off to war together, and served with courage and valor during WWII, came home, would marry and raise a family, and now in retirement fish the Connecticut River together, recalling the endearing moments of their lives.

(Left to right: John P. Gawlak, Edward J. Siecienski, John P. Cubeta)

But they rarely speak of their War experiences. Ed would receive the Silver Star for Heroic action on D-day. John Cubeta would receive the Bronze Star for Gallantry on Iwo Jima. John Gawlak would witness a Japanese suicide submarine (A. Kaiten) blow up the ammunition ship Uss Mt. Hood into a giant fireball, where no traces of the ship or crew were ever found. Five Friends from his home town were lost with that ship.

FISHING BUDDIES

John P. Gawlak and Albert "Ike" Ambressechio are long time fishing fiends and WWII veterans. Ike recently passed away from complications of a stroke. We would fish for trout in a remote pond in Bethlehem, CT. The pond was continually stocked by a nearby hatchery. Since the pond was private, we fished until it froze over. Ike was wounded many times as he was part of a crew of a Rescue Plane that evacuated heavily wounded casualties of island invasions in the pacific. The Hospital ships USS Mercy and USS Solace would treat other casualties when conditions became safer.

THE GAWLAK FAMILY

Jenny and Peter Gawlak, Kimberly and Charles Gawlak, Vincent and Catherine
Paradiso, Carol and John Gawlak, Patti and Thomas Gawlak

THE GRANDCHILDREN

Olivia, Annelise, Jeff, Billy, Nick, Brian, Joe, Mike, Jennifer, Natalie, Charlie, Emily